DISCLAIMER

The activities discussed in this book are inherently dangerous and should not be done by anyone.

The author wrote this book for the entertainment of himself and his readers, and not to encourage participation in the activities he describes. Furthermore, information in this book is based on the author's opinion, observations, and sometimes poetically exaggerated view of the world, and consequently should not be taken as fact.

If you feel compelled to try these activities despite this warning, we further suggest that you do not attempt them unless you are 100% willing to take full responsibility for any problems your actions might cause including potential damage to property, life, limb, and your own criminal record.

There is an implied ethic of personal responsibility for anyone who engages in "adventurous" or "dangerous" activities. The author expects that anyone who uses this handbook will adhere to that ethic.

The author, publisher, and contributors to this book accept no responsibility or liability for any actions or attitudes of anyone who uses this book and are consequently carrying no liability insurance related to this book.

THE
URBAN
ADVENTURE
HANDBOOK

Alan S. North

ILLUSTRATED BY
Charles K. Neifeld

TEN SPEED PRESS
Berkeley, California

ACKNOWLEDGMENTS

This book would not have been possible without the assistance and support from my friends and family. I am especially indebted to Donna Jaffe and Charles Neifeld for their creative input and insistent editorial contributions. I especially want to thank Charles Neifeld again for his illustrations and to Marty Chappell for his photographs. They both captured the essence of the urban adventure in their artistic contributions.

I appreciation everyone who read the text, made comments, modeled for photos, offered me the use of their adventure stories, provided adventuring expertise, provided encouragement, and otherwise helped in many ways. These people include Lisa Fink, Jim Gloystein, Beth Jordan, Peter Leeming, Keith Monroe, Robert Neifeld, John Newman, Antje Oehmichen, Dan Quinn, David Salvesen, Carole Taylor, Mike Weston, Steve Wheeler, and Russell Zeid.

Information contained in this book is for amusement purposes only. The publisher assumes no responsibility for anyone attempting any of the stunts contained within, legal or otherwise.

Copyright © 1990 by Alan S. North
All rights reserved. No part of this book may be reproduced in any form, except for brief reviews, without the written permission of the publisher.

1☺
TEN SPEED PRESS
P.O. Box 7123
Berkeley, California 94707

Cover design by Nancy Austin
Illustrations © 1990 by Charles K. Neifeld
All photographs © 1990 by Marty Chappell except the following:
Page 8, 34, 44a, 44d, 44e, 120 copyright © 1990 by Charles K. Neifeld
Page 37, 91, 116 copyright © 1990 by Alan S. North
Page 152 copyright © 1990 by Robert P. Neifeld

Library of Congress Cataloging in Publication Data
North, Alan S.
   The urban adventure handbook / Alan S. North ; illustrated by
Charles K. Neifield.
      p. cm.
   ISBN 0-89815-373-5
   1. Outdoor recreation—Humor. 2. Outdoor life—Humor. 3. Cities
and towns—Humor. I. Title.
PN6231.096N67 1990
818'.5407—dc20.   90-11077
                                                                CIP

Printed in the United States of America

1 2 3 4 5 - 94 93 92 91 90

TO THE BODIVOODOO

The first time I saw the Bodivoodoo I thought that he was a window washer. When I looked closer at the sparkly eyed bearded man smiling at me from the other side of the glass, I saw that he was in fact climbing the thirty-one-story structure. I raced to the roof to meet him, but there was no one in sight. The sky was blue and the air was warm. I walked the perimeter of the roof, peering over the edge and picking out landmarks from the skyline. I had never seen the city look so inviting before.

The next time I saw him I was riding my bicycle. I was on my way to a movie when I was passed by a fire truck with screaming sirens and flashing lights. The Bodivoodoo was on a bicycle drafting the fire truck. In the first instant I wasn't quite sure where I'd seen him. In the second instant I was just shocked to see him again. Next thing I knew I was in hot pursuit of the fire truck and its drafter. I couldn't catch him but had one of the most exciting bike rides of my life.

After that we kept running into each other all over town. Since then he has become my teacher, guide, and friend.

CONTENTS

adventure (n) **1:** an undertaking involving danger and unknown risks
2: an exciting and remarkable experience

adventure (vt) **1:** to expose to danger or loss: VENTURE **2:** to venture upon: TRY
(vi) **1:** to proceed despite danger or risk **2:** to take risk

---

* *Webster's Ninth New Collegiate Dictionary*
  (Springfield, MA: Merriam-Webster, 1981).

ADVENTURE IN THE URBAN ENVIRONMENT

Call of the Wild

Have you ever needed to go on a big adventure, but been stuck in the city? Have you ever seen those pictures of people climbing sheer rock walls, skiing down steep mountain couloirs, exploring deep underground caverns, or leaping into the air with a mile of sky below and a view of seven counties—and wished they were of you? Have you ever wished that you lived two hundred years ago when the country was young and the West called people like you to come and test their fiber? Have you ever felt like going out to find some excitement, but the art museums, pool halls, roller-skating rinks, movie theaters, and coffeehouses just wouldn't do? Have you ever wanted exhilaration that jogging in the park and a game of racquetball wouldn't deliver? Have you ever felt that the concrete-and-asphalt-covered world that you are spending your life in keeps you from your true essential nature as an adventurer? Then maybe it is time to explore **URBAN ADVENTURES.**

It is easy to start off on an **URBAN ADVENTURE.** Doing so requires very little time and, usually, no money. The **URBAN ADVENTURE** can be done alone or with a group of friends. It can be had during the day or night, weekday or weekend, rain or shine, any season. All you need is a creative view toward the sculpture that is all around you, a few free hours, and the will to be an adventurer.

What is Urban Adventure?

The verb *adventure* means to take a chance and to be at risk. Technically speaking, the **URBAN ADVENTURER** is one who sets out to venture into the unknown in an urban environment. Of course, depending on who you ask, this could include dining at a new restaurant, walking through a new neighborhood, seeing the opening of a new musical comedy, trying a tai chi or belly-dancing class at the YMCA, or simply talking with a stranger on the bus. Each of these activities may contain an element of adventure, and all may be worth doing. However, they don't conjure the bodily reaction you will have if you imagine yourself hanging by your fingertips one thousand feet up on a vertical wall, accelerating down a steep, forested, snow-covered slope on skis slightly faster than you can control, or free-falling down the face of a wave just inside the curl with a wall of water waiting to punish you for the slightest mistake. The first set of activities are urban, the second set are adventures.

Just the thought of a real adventure will make your body respond. Fear is important. Adventure is something to make your hands sweat, eyes open wide, heart pound, blood rush through your veins, hair stand on end, teeth chatter, knees knock, and throat tighten. You may gasp for breath. You will feel uncomfortable but exhilarated, with a sense of **WOW.**

Although adventure is a body-oriented experience, it is not *just* body oriented. Adventure happens when you push your body to the known limit, take one step beyond that, and then use all of your focused mental capacity in an attempt to recover.

Once you have entered the realm of adventure, you are already beyond what you had believed was "safe." Your objective becomes survival. You must gain control when you are out of control. Your mind and body must work together in harmony, or you will pay the price of failure. You will be absorbed in the moment, paying complete attention to what you are doing and what is going on around you. You may be scared. You may have doubts about your physical ability to succeed, your mental capacity to overcome difficulties, your determination to endure, and your sanity for allowing yourself to get into the situation in the first place.

Adventure is a deeply personal experience, even when undertaken as a group. What may be a grand adventure for one person may not be for another. Two people may be scaling a tower. The first person may be testing the limits of his skill and courage. He is on an adventure. The second person may find the same climb easy and routine. She may be having a good time, but she is not on an adventure.

URBAN ADVENTURES provide a chance to experience true adventure in an urban environment. They can propel you into an unknown, untamed, high-risk world within minutes of your front door. **URBAN ADVENTURES** include climbing on buildings, bicycle riding in traffic, balancing on slack chains, scaling high rises, exploring caverns beneath city streets, and more.

Going on **URBAN ADVENTURES** will change the way you see your urban environment. The structured, asphalt-and-concrete, developed world will become your wilderness playground. An old brick building will become a choreographer and teach you to dance in a vertical world. The blacktopped, potholed pavement will become a rapids-filled river enticing and challenging the deft navigator. A commuter-choking bridge will become a sculpture to climb. The smelly sewers beneath the city will become a Minoan labyrinth.

URBAN ADVENTURES are intentionally potentially dangerous. In contrast, most activities in our lives, such as walking down the street and driving a car, have minimal risks. For the most part, we ignore the risks. We lumber along, unconscious of the danger we are facing. What we miss is the feeling of exhilaration and aliveness that accompanies the realization of danger. We are lost in thoughts about our make-believe worlds and perform routine tasks that move us from one moment to the next. Our time passes, seldom punctuated by anything that stands out to let us know we are alive. However, when confronted straight on with imminent, life-threatening danger, we are shocked into acute awareness of our own mortality. We cling to life. We open our eyes, see the beauty of the day, marvel at the insignificant, rejoice in the mundane, and allow every moment to be full of meaning. When we are scared, we know we exist. Life, previously taken for granted, becomes the most cherished treasure.

Risk and Responsibility

"Never climb higher than you are willing to be wrong."
BODIVOODOO

All of the activities described in the **URBAN ADVENTURE HANDBOOK** involve taking calculated risks that have the potential to maim, kill, or lead to arrest. Anyone who tries any of these **URBAN ADVENTURES** should understand the potential risks and be willing to accept full responsibility for putting him- or herself in these situations.

There are physical risks. If you fall from a high place, you may get hurt or die. There are risks to property. In the process of having an **URBAN ADVENTURE,** you may destroy property, for which you may be liable. There are legal risks. Several techniques and activities described in the **URBAN ADVENTURE HANDBOOK** involve breaking traffic and trespassing laws, for which you may be apprehended and convicted.

You should consider the risks carefully. Never enter any risky situation without first assessing the severity of the risk, the likelihood of its occurrence, and your willingness to pay the consequences if you are wrong. Each person should make an individual assessment and decision because he or she will ultimately be responsible for the outcome.

When you accept risk, you accept responsibility. Assume that you happen to see a building that begs to be climbed. You scale protruding bricks to the second story. You are a little scared about being up so high and reach for the fire escape, assuming "safety." You do not test it before committing your weight. It is rusted. It breaks. You descend much faster than expected and break your arm. Who is responsible? The building owner is negligent for having a faulty fire escape. However, you were climbing the building. You were responsible for making sure all of the holds were safe. As an adventurer, your failure to climb safely is your own fault. Therefore, within the framework of this ethic, your reason for being on the fire escape precludes your right to seek damages from the building owner.

As an **URBAN ADVENTURER**, your successes, failures, pain, and glory are yours alone. You choose the activity and you own the outcome.

Safety

"The 'emergency landing' is constantly changing."
BODIVOODOO

Safety is an important element of adventuring precisely because the activity involves risks. There are two approaches to safety.

1. Abstinence

The first approach involves avoiding all potentially dangerous situations. Abstinence cannot guarantee safety, but it does reduce the probability of harmful accidents. Unfortunately, this tactic practically eliminates the possibility of having **URBAN ADVENTURES.**

2. Paying Attention and Exercising Judgment

The second approach involves consciousness and judgment. Most people who get hurt while doing dangerous things aren't paying complete attention to what they are doing.

You can usually have an injury-free adventure if you take a moment to evaluate all the available information about your activity before you begin. You will also want to make educated guesses about the relevant unknowable factors and reassess them along the way. Finally, proceed by acting on your assessment.

For example, when climbing a building, you will want to consider the following types of questions:

• Is the wall sturdy? Will the footholds or handholds break? Are they wet or slippery?

• What are the consequences of not going all the way to a safe stopping place? Is there a retreat?

• If you fall, would the landing be safe? How high up will you be? Is the landing surface smooth and clear like a sidewalk or grass or is it uneven with protruding objects—like fences, pipes, or rocks—that could hurt you?

• Is there any chance something external will effect your climb? Will something fall from above? Is the wind so strong it may blow you off?

• What about your own skill and endurance? Are you up to the challenge before you?

If you choose to adventure, be guided by the Bodivoodoo's maxim, "Never climb higher than you are willing to be wrong." Weigh the chance of failure against the consequence of failure. There may be a high cost to failure, but the chance of failing may be slim, for example, as when you climb a ladder on a high tower on a windless day. There may be a high chance of failure, but a low cost, as when you walk on a slack chain a few inches off a putting green. Both of these activities are relatively safe. On the other hand, walking a slack cable a hundred feet above the ground is not a safe activity because both consequences and likelihood of failure are high, unless you are very skillful at cable walking.

How to Find Adventure
in an Urban Environment

If you are like me, you tend to think of adventures taking place somewhere outside of the civilized world in the most extreme, stark, or exotic settings. Places that come to mind are vast deserts, high mountains, deep remote canyons, endless stretches of open water, raging torrents, and, in general, wild places beyond the reassuring grasp of human comfort and control.

Exotic locations enhance adventures. They offer rare beauty and enchanting surprises that enrich life. These surprises may even compensate for all the discomfort that tends to accompany adventurous journeys. But adventure is not about scenery. Adventure is about challenge.

URBAN ADVENTURES offer challenges similar to those of adventures found in wild places. Urban and wilderness adventures require use of the same skills and present the same deadly risks. **URBAN ADVENTURES** provide moments of fear and exhilaration in situations within, but beyond the control of, our highly structured world.

Skills and attributes necessary for most adventurous activities are: *(1) objective danger analysis, (2) route planning, (3) balancing, (4) self-confidence,* and *(5) committed maneuver execution.* Find an activity in an urban environment that requires these things and you will likely find an **URBAN ADVENTURE.**

1. *Objective danger analysis* should be the first step, and a continuing element, of all adventurous activities. An ice climber constantly assesses the weather, scrutinizes the quality of the ice, and tests each hold. Similarly, someone climbing a building must test each hold. Someone walking on a fence must be sure the fence is sturdy each step along the way and pay attention to which side has the preferable landing should he fall.

2. *Route planning* is both an initial and ongoing process in most adventure activities. A windsurfer watches the swells and wind direction to adjust the tack accordingly. The builderer scouts a general line to climb and often must plan each move to be positioned for the next. A bike rider in traffic must plan several swerving maneuvers ahead as he weaves in and out between slow-moving vehicles.

3. *Balancing* is the critical physical skill common to almost all human-powered adventure activities as well as to many nonhuman-powered activities. Balance, more than strength, is the key to graceful rock climbing, skiing, and surfing. Balancing in precarious places and under threatening circumstances attracts people who seek exhilaration and challenge. Ingenious new ways to test balance have created countless sports like logrolling, wire walking, and several types of wrestling. The challenge to balance is in our genes; ask any toddler. When you take that challenge to the extreme, you are likely to find adventure.

4. *Self-confidence* is believing in yourself and trusting that you are capable of getting yourself out of any jam that you get yourself into. Adventures occur when you have enough self-confidence to perform at the edge of your ability. Self-confidence increases with the practice of living on that edge. Over time, an adventurer gains the confidence to move ever closer to his performance edge even as that boundary is expanding.

5. *Committed maneuver execution* often determines whether an action will be a success or a failure. The skier who does not commit to a turn will often fall backward. The climber who does not trust his feet will not move up. The jumper who hesitates at take-off will fall short of the mark. But the adventurer who visualizes a successful assent and approaches each move free of doubt or ambiguity usually succeeds. When the mind is programmed the body will follow.

This handbook describes how and where to practice these **URBAN ADVENTURE** skills.

The Law

"Follow it or expect it to follow you."
BODIVOODOO

The distinction between law and justice is complex. In general, our legal system does the best it can to promote a just society. However, sometimes the law falls short of justice in favor of what society believes to be the greater good. For example, lax environmental pollution laws are based on the common misconception that the economy would suffer if pollution-control requirements were strict enough to guarantee that everyone could drink clean water and breathe clean air. At other times, the law overextends authority in a restrictive manner. Many vice laws fall into this category, as do some bans on free speech, religion, and political expression.

It is best if we obey all laws. However, as you pursue **URBAN ADVENTURES,** you will likely make some minor transgressions, particularly in the areas of trespassing and traffic regulations. Some of these laws tend to be a by-products of our overprotective, litigious society. Injury and damage will result from these transgressions only when you are careless.

Should you decide that certain laws are overrestrictive, be sure that you continue to follow the spirit and intent of those laws. Make sure that your adventuring does not burden other people. The Bodivoodoo says that adventuring is best when "no one knows and no one cares." Be respectful of other people and their property. Avoid causing injury to other people and their property. If you willfully or inadvertently cause injury, you should pay for the damage.

Practically speaking, the letter of the law applies only to those who break a law and are proven guilty before a court. The best way to avoid suffering legal consequences for your transgressions is to not get caught. Other, less-reliable methods include, quick talking, luck, bribery (not recommended), and good legal council. Many law enforcement officers choose not to issue citations to polite urban adventurers if a crime has created neither damage nor victim.

Should you be convicted of a crime such as one you may commit in pursuit of an **URBAN ADVENTURE**, expect to pay a small fine and to be confronted with the embarrassing truth about your own adolescent nature.

BUILDERING

A middle-aged portly gent in an anonymous brown suit pushed through the bank doors into the sunlight. His breathing was labored as he tilted his head back and squinted toward the Bodivoodoo high on a column, reaching for the summit scroll.

The stress on the banker's face reached the Bodivoodoo well before his word.

"What are you doing up there?" demanded the banker.

The Bodivoodoo sensed that the man did not really want to know.

"Coming down," the climber said calmly.

Buildering is the activity of climbing buildings.

Buildering derives its origin from the sport of bouldering, the act of climbing on boulders. Rock climbers and mountaineers boulder (do bouldering) to keep in shape and to hone their climbing techniques. Some climbers prefer boulders over other climbing mediums. Boulders occur in more places than mountains or climbing crags, which makes them more accessible to climbers. Because boulders are not very high, climbers feel free to attempt extremely difficult climbing moves with little threat of getting hurt.

When rock climbers and mountaineers find themselves living in urban areas, unable to get to mountains, crags, or boulders, they start climbing buildings. Climbers have found that buildings offer superb climbing challenges, as well as being much more accessible than traditional climbing areas.

The builderer, one who does buildering, climbs the external architectural features of a building. The builderer can move up, down, or across a wall by progressively

moving his hands or feet on the building's features in the desired direction. This is done without the aid of special climbing equipment; no ropes or ascending machines are used.

Excellent buildering can occur within several feet of the ground. Fortunately, this allows for exciting climbing challenges with minimal physical risk.

The Medium

Buildering can be performed on a variety of structural materials including brick, cinder block, concrete, wood, and metal. If the building is structurally sound and buildering is performed correctly, none of these materials will be worse for the wear if climbed upon.

One favorite building material for builderers is brick. Some brick facades have randomly placed protruding bricks that make excellent hand- and footholds. The holds can range in size from the width of a brick to the width of dime.

Stone buildings, rare in most urban areas, offer exquisite buildering. Buildering on stone is a cross between buildering on brick and climbing an actual rock wall. Surfaces are irregular, uneven, and often sloping. The buildings are usually grand, majestic structures housing stodgy, authoritative institutions. But a stone facade can have an authority of its own, beckoning the builderer to scamper on the wall, light and free, like a lizard.

More and more buildings are being constructed out of concrete. Concrete expands and contracts as temperature changes. Consequently, long vertical and/or horizontal cracks must be built into the facade to allow for the expansion and contraction. Unfortunately, these cracks are seldom wide enough for use by a builderer. But the good news is that vertical cracks of varying widths are often added to concrete buildings just to offset the visual monotony of the building material. These cracks can facilitate excellent climbing.

Wood structures are good for climbing, particularly when they have ledge systems on the walls. These ledge systems can serve any function from structural support to decorative trim. Design accoutrements may or may not be strong enough to support climbing activity; builderers should be sensitive to the potential fragility of the material.

Types of Walls

A building's exterior architecture, more than any other single factor, determines whether it is a good climb. Most buildings can be climbed and climbed safely. The **URBAN ADVENTURER** is motivated by walls that look interesting and say "climb me."

ALLEY WALLS

Appreciation of alley-wall buildering is acquired. Although alley ways do not usually offer expansive views of the urban landscape, they do appeal to the **URBAN ADVENTURER** who is interested in urban wildlife. They are great places to see spiders, cockroaches, ants, earwigs, termites, mice, and rats.

The walls of alleyways between residential buildings are filled with windows and wastewater pipes. These are very easy to climb. Window ledges occur at even intervals of one story. Many windows have some form of sturdy trim that allows you to stand on top of the window area and reach the next window sill.

The obvious things to climb on alleyway walls are the drain pipes and rain gutter pipes. I personally never trust these pipes. They are often old, worn, rusted, or made of materials like clay that are not designed for external stress. If you decide that you must climb on the pipes, be sure to exert force only in a downward direction. If force is exerted outwardly, the pipes could break or pull away from the wall.

While in the alley you may notice that many buildings have back staircases. Although these are not much fun to walk up and down on when you are taking out the garbage, they are fun to climb inverted. Gripping the steps from underneath and pulling yourself up, you will get a great upper-body workout on the inverted ladder.

AIR AND LIGHT SHAFTS

Those people who really like buildering in alleyways may also like buildering in air and light shafts. The two settings offer many similar experiences, including extensive climbing on the outside of window sills. Air and light shafts are ideal places to practice stemming or stretching a leg to a foothold off to the side. The view is limited, though potentially interesting from an anthropological perspective. This is a great way to get to know the people in your building.

VICTORIANS

Buildering on Victorian-style buildings is especially interesting to those who like climbing on wooden sculptures. Victorians are commonly identified by their bay windows, high ceilings, and carved exterior trim. The bay windows offer good resting places, which are needed because high ceilings mean long distances between floors.

GREEK REVIVAL

Buildings with Roman or Greek Revival architecture are great for buildering because of their scale and because they tend to be made of solid material: typically stone or some aggregate concrete. A variety of climbing problems can be found on columns, friezes, and sculpted scrolls.

EDUCATIONAL AND INSTITUTIONAL BUILDINGS

Religious, educational, and institutional buildings come in a variety of sizes, architectural styles, and building materials. It is precisely because they tend to be varied that they are likely candidates for good buildering.

DOWNTOWN HIGH RISE OFFICES

In general, downtown high rises are not particularly good for buildering. However, sometimes a building will have a climbable crack system that goes straight up for hundreds of feet or some other features that beg for buildering. Most of the time the features are very uniform in character and go from the bottom to the top of the structure.

I personally seldom builder up high rises beyond the second or third story. By then I've worked out the technical climbing challenge and am confronted with a potential fall with consequences beyond the value of continuing up.

If there is a climbing route that goes all the way to the top and that route demands to be climbed, it is often better to use some equipment for backup. Techniques to enhance the safety of these higher climbs are discussed in the chapter titled "Going High," page 125.

HUMAN-MADE CLIMBING WALLS

There growing number are of human-made climbing walls in urban areas. Climbers have been using high-grade epoxies to glue small rocks onto otherwise unadorned concrete public infrastructure walls such as freeway underpasses, road-supporting walls, and concrete water channels. Often these climbing walls are made under overhangs so that they will be dry places for workouts in the rain. Santa Cruz, California, has two human-made climbing walls that offer excellent climbing challenges.

Technique

Basic buildering techniques are fundamentally the same as techniques used for any other type of climbing. In essence, there are six principles to remember.

1. *Use your feet as much as possible.* When you are climbing, push with your legs. While not moving, keep as much of your weight on your feet as possible. Your leg

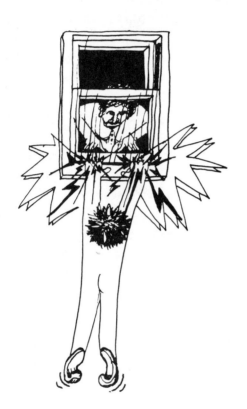

muscles are much stronger than your arm muscles. No remotely normal human being can continually pull himself up all day long with his arms. Many people can barely do one pull-up. However, most anyone can climb hundreds of stairs.

Use you arms and hands primarily to keep yourself from falling backward and to offer backup protection while you are moving your feet. Hands and arms tire easily. There is no reason to overuse them by pulling yourself up and hanging by them. Very little arm strength or energy is required to hold yourself, except when climbing overhangs or laybacks. You need to hold on only enough to stay on. Holding on any tighter wastes energy that you may need later.

2. *Keep your body away from the wall.* The proper body position is to be upright and back from the wall. If you are pressed flat against the wall you will not be able to see your next hold and you will not be able to move.

3. *Keep three trusted points on the wall.* The most secure position is always with two good footholds and two good handholds. However, to move to another hold, you must release a hand or a foot. Only move one hand or foot at a time. Be sure to leave the remaining appendages on secure holds. Your chances of recovering if a hold breaks, or if you slip off a hold while in the middle of a move, depends on how many holds you have left. If you are moving one appendage and a second slips,

you have two remaining holds to catch yourself. However, if you are moving two appendages and a third slips, you have one hold left to prevent you from falling.

4. *Move your feet first.* If you are climbing up, look for your next foothold first, step up on it second, and move your hands up third. If you are stable, there is seldom a reason to look for new handholds prior to stepping up on your next foothold. Once you have the new foothold, your body position will be so different that the hands must be changed anyway.

Generally, you will want to first move your appendages that are furthest away from the direction you are climbing. Think about the inchworm pulling itself by scooting its back end up to its front and then thrusting its front end forward. To climb up, move your feet first and then your arms. To climb down, first move your hands as low as possible, then move your feet. To traverse, move the trailing hand and foot prior to moving the leading pair.

5. *Stay relaxed.* Relaxation is essential for enjoyable and sustained climbing. Hands should grip the handholds only as hard as they need to. The foot should be relaxed on the foothold, with the heel down even as the toes are gripping. Standing on your tiptoes only leads to calf convulsions, commonly known as "sewing machine leg." The mind should be relaxed as well. There is no reason to be vexed while buildering or climbing in general. There is enough time to think through moves, look around, and enjoy being on a vertical world.

6. *Move gracefully.* Locate holds visually. Do not scrape your feet up and down walls. Scraping will not help you find holds; it will only wear your shoes and leave marks on the walls.

Place your hand or foot on a new hold smoothly and in a controlled manner. It is best not to lunge for a hold. You want to be able to test the hold. If you don't like the hold, you will want to be able to move your hand or foot back to its original secure position.

Remember, climbing is dance.

Recognizing Holds

The trick to climbing anything is finding someplace to put your hands and feet that will enable your ascent. The places where you put your hands and feet are called "holds." Recognizing holds is the art of climbing; using holds is the craft.

There are two basic types of holds: footholds and handholds. The major distinction between a foothold and a handhold is the part of the body that is placed on the building feature. If you use your foot on a hold, it is a foothold; if you use your hand, it's a handhold. Within these broad categories are several variations. Distinctions between different types of hand- and footholds are based on size, shape, and how they are used.

All holds are formed by a discontinuity in the building surface. This can be the result of a change of shape, a change of direction on the surface, the joining of different materials, structural irregularities, building degradation, or defects. Any discontinuity may be a potential hold if you can figure out how to use it.

Testing Holds

To test a handhold, first make sure that your other hand and both of your feet are securely on the building. Move your hand to the new hold. Gradually apply the force to the hold in the same direction that you intend to use it; pull up on the hold if you intend to pull up on it, or push down on the hold if you intend to push down on it. As you apply pressure, look, feel, and listen for any signs that the hold may not accept your weight or directional pull. These signs can include movement, cracking, sponginess, or general discomfort in the bottom of your stomach. Another method is to strike the hold with your hand. Strike gently at first to be sure that you do not destroy the building's feature. Trust your intuition. If you do not trust the hold, remove your hand and find another. Otherwise, gradually commit yourself to using the hold, making sure that you can reverse the move at any time until you feel secure and ready to move another hand or foot.

To test a foothold, follow the same procedure as above. Make sure both hands and the other foot are secure. Apply all of your weight to the new foothold gradually in the testing process.

Using Protrusions and Other Horizontal Handholds

Horizontal holds are used by placing the hands or fingers on the hold and applying downward force. If the hold is above your shoulders, pulling is required. If the hold is below your shoulders, pushing is required.

Horizontal holds can be flat, incut, or sloping. Incut holds are the easiest to grip because you can wrap your hand or fingers around them. Sloping holds are the hardest to use because your hands will tend to slide off of them.

Edge

Edges are the smallest holds, allowing only part of your fingers on them. There are two finger positions for using edges. For the smallest edges, your fingers should come into contact with the hold from a vertical position. Imagine trying to dig your fingernails into the hold. For slightly larger edges, your fingertips can lie flat on the hold with your fingers angled up and away from the wall.

Ledges are wide enough to place at least two joints of your middle finger on. However, they are not wide enough to climb on top of without holding on to something above. Generally, fingers are placed on the ledge such that finger joints are directly above the end of the ledge. Sometimes more of the hand is put on the ledge if possible.

Mantelshelves are ledges that can be climbed on without the use of any holds from above. The manteling technique is typically used to ascend window ledges or sills.

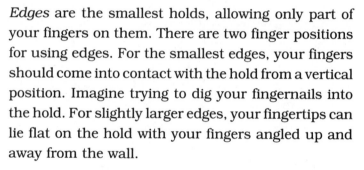

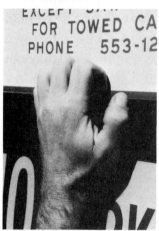

Fingernail edge

Pinch grip

Pinch gripping means squeezing a protruding hold between the thumb and fingers. Pinch gripping can be used to supplement an existing handhold, making a shaky handhold more secure.

Pinch grip

To mantel:

1. Get yourself up as high as you can by holding the shelf and working your feet up on the wall.

2. Place your hands palms-down on the shelf. Sometimes it helps to swing your hands around so that the fingers are facing inward.

3. Push down, extending your arms.

4. Place one foot up on the shelf.

5. Shift your weight onto the foot and stand up.

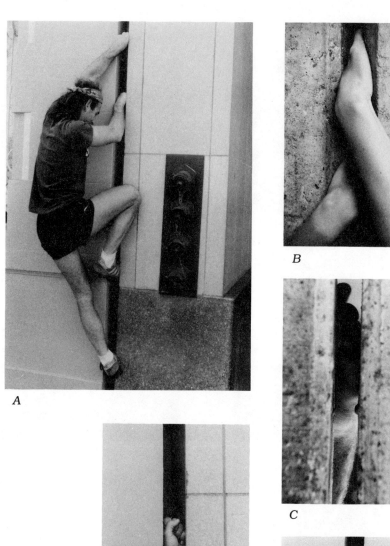

A

B

C

E

D

(A) Climbing a jam crack, (B) Jamming a thin crack,
(C) Finger stack, (D) Hand jam, (E) Fist jam.

Cracks, Holes, and Other Vertical Handholds

A vertical hold occurs in the space between two vertical surfaces. The hold used by filling the space, or jamming. When the hold is jammed properly, the fingers or hands become wedged tightly between the two vertical surfaces as downward pressure is applied. This often requires applying a rotational force to torque the hand or fingers, which may be painful.

- *Thin cracks* are many people's favorite size. They are the width of your fingers. Sometimes they are very narrow so that only the tips of certain fingers will fit in them. Other times they are very wide, and your fingers will fit in up to the last joints. To use a finger crack, it is usually best to place your hand upside down, thumb down, with your fingers as deep in the crack as possible. Applying a downward pull will twist the fingers and torque them in tighter to secure a solid grip.

- *Off-size finger cracks* are some of the hardest to use. Off-size means that your fingers will wiggle around insecurely inside the crack, but your hand will not fit. Place your hand upside-down, with the palm side of your thumb against one vertical wall and your index and middle fingers between the other wall and your thumb. Torque to lock.

- *Hand cracks* are very secure. They range in size from just large enough to allow your hand in the crack, up to the thumb, to the width of your fist. Fill the crack by opposing your thumb (bringing it in toward your little finger) and by cupping your hand. A hand crack hold is often more secure when the hand is placed in it with the thumb facing down.

- *Fist cracks* are the size of your fist. Fill the crack by expanding your fist and moving the thumb outward, away from your little finger.

- *Off-width cracks* are larger than your fist and smaller than your chest. They are particularly awkward and require placing your arms in some filthy places. Hold yourself in an off-width crack by placing one arm in the crack with your palm against the wall you are facing and your elbow and shoulder braced against the wall behind you. (Use little edges if possible.) Place your other hand upside down on the corner of the wall in front of you and push away from your body. Move your feet up, get some footholds, and move your arms up again. Luckily, urban off-width cracks can usually be climbed using a layback technique, so don't worry about this one.

Foot Placement

There are five basic types of foot placements: edging, smearing, jamming, heel-toe, and foot stacks.

- *Edging* is the technique used to place a foot on small, clearly defined, flat or incut holds. Imagine curling your toe around the hold. Place the big toe on the hold and try to force your foot into the vertical wall.

    Edging can also be done with the outside of the foot. This technique is less secure and requires wider holds.

- *Smearing* is the technique used to place a foot on rounded holds, edges too small for edging techniques, slight bumps, coarse areas on the wall, and other poorly defined holds. To smear, place the ball of your foot flat on the hold, imagine curling your toes around the hold, have faith, and stand. The friction between your foot and the wall will often be enough to enable your assent.

- *Jamming* is the technique used for vertical cracks. Place your foot straight into the crack with the sole vertical, big toe up, little toe down. Then twist your foot to make the sole horizontal. In other words, slip your foot into the crack the narrow way and expand it by torquing your foot toward the wide way. If the crack is very narrow, you may only be able to get the tip of your shoe in. Depending on the size of the crack, jamming can be so secure that your foot will get stuck.

- *Heel-toe* technique is used for vertical cracks that are wider than the width of your foot. Place your foot in the crack horizontally. Rotate your foot laterally on the horizontal plane so that the toe is touching one vertical wall and the heel is touching the other. I generally prefer the outer toe and inner heel for this technique but inner toe and outer heel also works well.

- *Foot-stacking* technique is used for vertical cracks that are wider than the length of your foot. Place one foot against one wall. With the second foot, use the heel-toe technique between the first foot and the other wall. It is also possible to heel-toe both feet against each other and the respective walls.

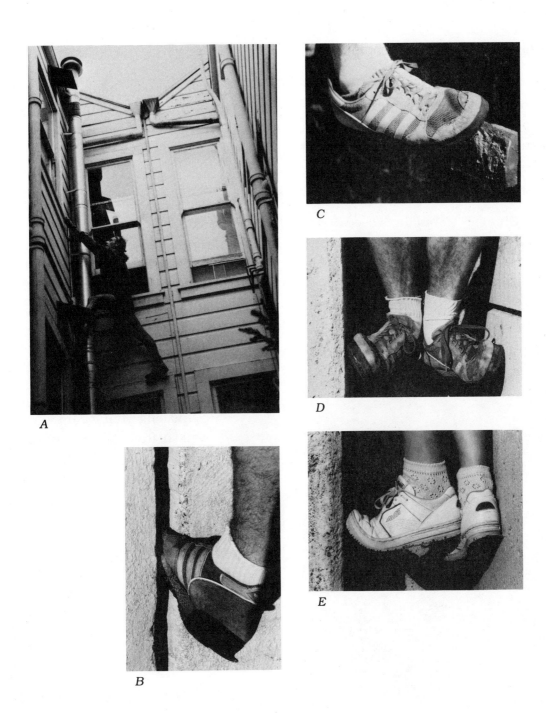

(A) Using an outside edge, (B) Foot jam, (C) Edging,
(D) and (E) Foot-stacking techniques.

Opposing Pressure Techniques

Several buildering techniques rely on pressure exerted simultaneously in opposing directions. For example, the hands may be working against the feet, or the two feet may push the body in opposite ways. The net result of opposing pressure can be secure buildering where no obvious conventional holds exist.

CHIMNEYING

Chimney technique is used in vertical cracks that are wide enough to fit the body. This type of crack is often created by the space between two buildings. To hold yourself in a chimney, wedge yourself between two walls. Done properly, this technique makes it almost impossible to fall out of a chimney, which is why I often choose chimney climbs when I want to climb high above the pavement.

Squeeze chimney

To ascend a chimney:

1. Secure yourself by wedging your upper body. This can be done by placing your palms on the wall in front of you and your elbows on the wall behind, or by pushing each hand against one wall.

2. Move your lower body up as high as you can. In wider chimneys you can move straight up. In narrow or "squeeze" chimneys, you will have to move up to the side. Use the flexibility in your back and hips for this maneuver.

3. Wedge your lower body in the higher position. This can be

done by placing your feet on the wall behind you and your knees on the wall in front, your feet on the wall in front of you and your behind on the wall in back, or each foot on a different wall.

4. Move your upper body up. With the lower body secure, you can straighten to an upright position. You are ready to repeat the process.

STEMMING

Stemming, sometimes called "bridging," involves extending each leg to the side to apply pressure against a vertical wall, vertical edge, or smear hold. It is typically used in corners or for extremely wide chimney problems.

I often use the stemming technique to simplify climbs. For example, while using a hand jam in a corner crack created by two very close buildings, I might stem out and place a foot on the exterior trim of a window as a means of resting in the middle of the climb.

LAYBACK

The layback technique involves pulling yourself into a corner with your hands while pushing yourself away from it with your feet. Typically this technique is used when there is a vertical crack that opens perpendicular to a wall that extends beyond the crack opening. A likely place to find this is where two buildings that do not quite touch extend outward different lengths. To ascend using the layback technique, walk your feet up the wall while pulling yourself toward the wall using the corner.

UNDERCLINGING

Underclinging is a technique that is using upside-down horizontal holds—typically an upside-down ledge or edge. Underclings are similar to laybacks in that you use opposing pressure between your hands and feet. To use an undercling, pull up on the undercling hold and push with the feet. Underclinging is particularly useful on overhangs above walkways.

Traversing

To traverse means to move across a building. Traversing can be done high or low on a wall. It is the best way to get a lot of buildering done with a minimum of danger.

Getting Down

Getting down is not much of a problem for most builderers. Since ropes and special safety hardware are not used, builderers seldom go higher than they are willing to downclimb, jump, or fall. However, you should always plan your descent if you are climbing up a building.

There are several ways to get off buildings. The preferred method is usually to climb down the way you got up.

If reversing the route is not possible, there could be an alternative, easier downclimbing route. You may be able to get to a tree or another building with an easier descent. Many buildings have fire escapes. Some have roof doors.

If none of those suggestions works, you have neglected part of your responsibility as an **URBAN ADVENTURER.** Call for help and get arrested for trespassing.

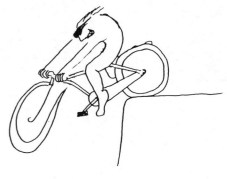

Safety and Special Risks

Buildering is a potentially dangerous activity. Caution should be observed whenever climbing anything. Difficult moves do not make a particular buildering problem dangerous. No one ever got hurt climbing. People get hurt when they suddenly stop climbing, fall for a while, and hit a solid surface.

1. Don't fall unless you have a good landing. There are many aspects to a good landing. The best landings are soft, uniform surfaces like sand or grass. Poor landings typically have irregular surfaces. Be aware of hidden obstructions. Falling on rocks or other obstructions, such as sprinkler heads, can cause you to break an ankle. The falling distance also determines the quality of a landing. All other things being equal, short falls have safer landings than long falls. Finally, your body position is important. If you do not want to get hurt, don't land on your head or with your ankle twisted or tucked under your body.

The Bodivoodoo says:
Better to downclimb than jump.
Better to jump than fall.
Better to fall short than far.
If you are high up, better not fall.

---

2. Use extra care when climbing on poor-quality building materials. Unsafe buildering walls include rotten wood, exposed sharp metal edges, exfoliating brick or concrete, unsound structures, very rusted barbed wire, and building materials that will not support force exerted by the builderer (such as some thin trim). It is much easier to stay on a wall if the wall stays intact.

3. Beware of what is falling from above. While on a wall, you are very vulnerable to flying debris cast off by unconscious workers, irate tenants, reactionary landlords, and childish pranksters.

4. Know your limitations. Buildering safety lies primarily in the judgment of the climber. Push your climbing limits when the consequences of failure will be benign. As the consequences of falling become increasingly harsh, you should take fewer chances.

5. Beware of arrest. If caught buildering, you could be convicted of trespassing and/or charged with other crimes.

Etiquette

• When climbing past windows it is not polite to look in. This is especially true if there is something interesting to see.

• Try not to leave any marks on walls, especially if you are buildering someplace where you may not want to get caught. The one exception is when buildering on a wall that is well established for climbing with the consent of the owner.

• If a building management authority asks you to get off of the building, it is best to acquiesce. Agree and leave the site promptly before the law arrives. If you are on a public or corporately owned building, you can always return later when no one is there to bother you, and, correspondingly, you will bother no one.

• It is better not to climb under another builderer. You may make him nervous and cause him to fall on you.

• If you are climbing above another builderer and using his handholds as footholds, try not to step on his fingers.

• Don't start climbing in the line of another builderer's traverse. If you do, be sure to move before she gets there. A good rule of thumb is that the first person on the wall has the right-of-way. Stepping off the wall for a rest forfeits the right-of-way.

• Don't tell other builderers that the big, obvious hold is "off-route" (not part of the climb) unless they are asking you for route information.

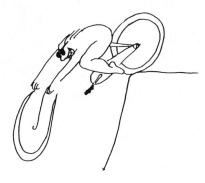

Equipment

Buildering *requires* no special equipment.

Chalk

Some builderers use gymnastic chalk to dry their hands. Holds tend to get slippery on buildings that get a lot of climbing use. A little moisture on the fingers can make you slip off small, smooth holds. In these instances, dusting your hands with chalk helps.

Some people also use chalk to help them see where they've been after they are done. This may help to elevate a faltering ego.

The disadvantage of chalk is that other people, too, can see where you have been. For other builderers, this shows the route and thereby makes it easier. The route-finding part of their adventure has been significantly diminished. For building owners, this proves that people are climbing their buildings.

Clothing

Clothing should enhance free movement. Loose-fitting clothing works great. Bright colors are preferred by those who want to be seen. Black is preferred by those who builder at night, especially if engaged in economic pursuits.

Shoes

Rock-climbing shoes are best. However, a good pair of tight-fitting sneakers works as well under most circumstances. Bare feet and sandals have been used successfully. Wing tips and high heels are not recommended except in the most extreme circumstances.

Buildering with My Cousin Chuckles in Chico

Pablo and I were visiting my cousin Chuckles up in Chico one spring. Chuckles is a real buildering maniac. He was showing us all of his favorite routes around campus. It's mostly old protruding brick up there, some real nice stuff.

Well, in the evening, we were walking by this old brick theater building. Chuckles noticed that the third-story window was open. There was a light on. Herb Caen, a San Francisco newspaper columnist, was speaking inside. It looked inviting, so we decided to go in . . . through the window, of course.

It was easy to climb on those bricks. Chuckles and I scampered up the theater wall while Pablo down below (always up for the spirit of adventure, though wary of actual danger), kept saying, "Do you think its safe?", "I don't know," and "It looks kind of high to me."

We went through the window, scouted for security guards, and looked for seats. The place was packed. There were no seats. We shuffled around and found an innocuous place to sit on the steps. After about five minutes, we knew we were safe. Herb was in fine form, but we weren't all that interested. We decided to go to the first-floor bathroom and open the window so Pablo could join us.

Chuckles hopped out of the window. After a few minutes he returned with Pablo. I don't know if Pablo was nervous about sneaking in or what, but he announced that he intended to sit in one of the stalls for a while.

Chuckles and I walked out through the doorway as a campus security cop walked in.

"You boys just come in through the window?" He asked.

I told the truth and said, "No."

He offered us an escort to the outside door, which we gratefully accepted.

As we walked through the doorway, he said, "Hold it one minute," so we started running.

We hit the street and split up. I ducked into an alley that led to an art studio.

The cop didn't follow me. I hid out for about half an hour in the studio and watched some artists blow glass.

The cop chased Chuckles downtown, calling for assistance on his radio. He was gaining on Chuckles, so Chuckles hopped a fence. The cop followed. Trapped in a restaurant's back patio, Chuckles saw a crack between two buildings in the yard's far corner. As the cop topped

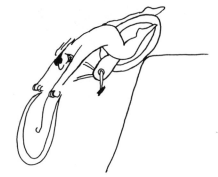

the fence, Chuckles started to layback the corner. Like a scared squirrel on amphetamines, Chuckles was two stories up the crack before the cop reached the corner. The cop couldn't follow.

Chuckles was soon on the roofs of a central downtown block. He heard sirens.

The block was surrounded, with several cops on each corner. Chuckles found an air duct to hide in. Twenty minutes later, he heard cops on the roofs making a systematic search of every nook and cranny. He shrank down as far as he could and did not move.

The cops had been on the roof for an hour and a half when they got to his hiding place. He quit breathing. They shone their flashlight in. He could feel the beam above his head. But they didn't stick their head in that dark hole. Too many spiders, Chuckles guessed.

As the footsteps moved away, Chuckles knew he was safe. He just had to wait.

BALANCING

"The best view of both sides is closest to the edge."
BODIVOODOO

Our ancestors were wild beings who lived by their instincts under the sun and stars with occasional hunger and cold to sharpen their wits and will. However, they were also social beings who banded together for mutual safety and comfort. Today, as urban and suburban dwellers, we are estranged from our natural habitat. We live in climate-controlled electric caves and no longer see the stars. Cold and hunger have been replaced by wonderful amenities that dull our instincts. Our will to survive has lost connection with its foundation, has been distorted, and is expressed through excessive behaviors.

Sometimes the wild person within us claws at our innards and screams to be set free into the lost, untamed world of our ancestors. The great challenge of urban life is to give the inner wild-person a voice without disrupting the rest of our lives. One way to strike that balance is to have a balance-oriented **URBAN ADVENTURE.**

Games in the wilderness that depend on balance abound. Skiing, surfing, and rock climbing are a few examples. In urban environments, human-made barriers, including fences, walkway hand railings, and chains across parking lots, offer some of the best places to use balancing skills.

Balance activities challenge the adventurer to perform the impossible. The challenge is against oneself. It requires tremendous concentration and, consequently, offers a great form of meditation. Single-mindedness is necessary to stay on a delicate balance. As any kid who has walked a railroad track knows, feedback is instantaneous; when you lose your focus . . . you fall off.

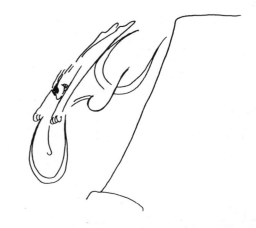

Balance activities are soothing. When you step on a slack chain, the rest of the world goes away. There is only you and the chain. You externalize the internal process of centering and achieve tranquility. You walk above the ground.

The Medium

There are three basic types of balance mediums: movable objects, fixed rails, and single-point balances.

Movable Objects

Movable objects are the focus of countless balance-oriented games. You can amuse yourself for hours by trying to stand on any cylindrical or spherical object. Two movable objects, slack chains and cables, are actually built into the urban landscape. Chains and cables typically act as barriers. They are often found across parking lots and driveways. They are almost always low to the ground (below waist high).

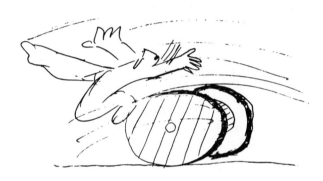

SLACK CHAIN CHARACTERISTICS

Every chain has a different combination of characteristics that determines the quality of the walk. For me, the ideal chain is strong, light, long, slack, laterally stable at both ends, not prone to rotations, void of dangling appendages, and bouncy. However, any chain may be fun to walk on if it is secure at both ends, will not break while you are standing on it, and has a safe landing for when you fall off.

1. *Strength.* Chain strength applies to the whole system, including the chain, the anchoring post or wall, and the connection between the two.

   The force you exert on a chain is much greater than your weight. The Chain Stress Analysis Formula shows how the chain's geometry magnifies the tension your weight exerts on the chain anchor points.

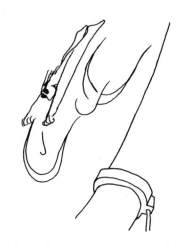

CHAIN STRESS ANALYSIS FORMULA

This formula allows you to calculate the amount of force on a chain's anchor points when you are standing in its exact middle and creating the greatest tension.

Assume the chain anchor points are level.

w =   your weight
c =   the chain's weight
l =   the length of the chain if stretched
h =   the vertical distance between the chain where you are standing and the anchor point level
T =   the tension at anchor point in the direction of the chain

$$T = \frac{l(w + c)}{2h}$$

Example: If you weigh 150 pounds, the chain weighs 25 pounds, the chain is 30 feet long, and the center point of the chain is 1.5 feet below the end points while you are on it, then

$$T = \frac{30 \times (150 + 25)}{2 \times 1.5}$$

$$T = 1{,}750 \text{ pounds}$$

This calculation does not include the additional force you would generate by "pushing down" or "bouncing" on the chain. If by bouncing you generated twice your body mass in force, the tension at the anchor points would be:

$$T = \frac{30 \times (300 + 25)}{2 \times 1.5}$$

$$T = 3{,}250 \text{ pounds}$$

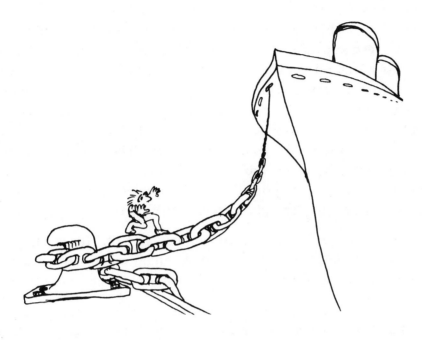

2. *Chain mass.* Chain walkers adjust their balance on the chain two ways: by moving their appendages, and by moving the chain. Light chains are easier to move than heavy chains, making them more responsive to the walker.

3. *Chain length.* Long chains have more consistent swing over a greater distance than do short chains. The center of a chain is easier to walk than the ends. Long chains have proportionally more distance that exhibits center dynamics (long even swings like big ocean swells) and less distance that exhibits end dynamics (short choppy swings like the agitated water inside a washing machine) than do short chains.

4. *Slackness.* Some chains are slack and others are taut. A chain's slackness is what gives it play. Slack chains are lively and more responsive to body movement, and they swing freely under your feet. As a chain becomes increasingly taut, it acts more like a fixed rail.

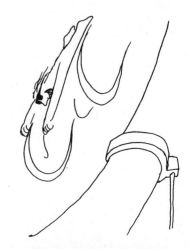

5. *Lateral stability.* Lateral stability at the ends depends on how chains are secured. Some chains have periodic supports running their length. These are often short support posts used to keep a very slack chain from touching the ground. Typically, a long chain fencing off a large lot will be constructed this way. Although the chain may be continuous, from the chain walker's perspective, its length is equal to the distance between supports. Sometimes a chain will run freely between support segments. As you stand on the chain, all of the slack from all of the other segments will migrate to your section. This itself is not a problem. Problems arise when the posts holding up the chain do not provide it with lateral stability. Sometimes the chain will run through a large ring that allows a lot of lateral motion as you swing on the chain. Other times the posts themselves will be loose and flip-flop side to side as the chain swings. This type of lateral instability at the chain's functional ends distorts a chain's uniform harmonic qualities and makes balance more difficult, or challenging, depending on your perspective.

6. *Rotation.* Some chains will rotate or roll under your foot. This is mostly the result of the shape of the link and how twisted the chain was when it was installed. If a chain is prone to rolling, anticipate the roll and let it occur prior to placing your foot.

7. *Bounciness.* Bouncy chains are a rare treat for chain walkers who like lively chains. Bounciness is caused by elasticity along the line of force. This can occur when the ends of the chain are attached to the anchor with an elastic material such as nylon rope. Bounciness can also occur if a chain is attached to an elastic object. For example, some chains are attached to metal posts that give, or are springy, when under horizontal stress.

8. *Dangling appendages.* Some chains have metal objects hanging from them that interfere with the natural harmonic swinging motion of the chain. For example, some chains have "No Parking" signs hanging from their centers. The dangling sign will respond to chain motion in a delayed manner and continue swinging after the chain has stopped. The disruption in the uniform swinging motion of the chain can throw the walker off balance, thus adding to the challenge.

The Difference Between a Slack Chain and a Cable

There is little difference between walking a slack chain and walking a slack cable. Chains are made of independent interlocking pieces of solid metal, which promote lateral flexibility. Cables are made of interdependent continuous strands of flexible metal. Chains tend to be more fluid and lively, cables easier to walk. Cables are less laterally flexible, which makes them more stable and sluggish. However, cables have more elasticity than chains, which can provide a little bounce. Very thin cables act more like chains than like thick cables because of their lighter weight and flexibility. However, thin cables stretch when weighted and tend to slip out from underfoot.

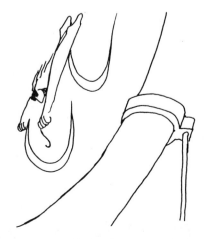

Fixed Rails

Fixed rails are any ridged structures of narrow width; such as railroad tracks, fences, bridge guardrails, and walkway handrails. "Narrow width" is subjective. Defining something as narrow depends on both the circumstances and the person making the assessment. A one-foot-wide steel beam lying on the ground may not seem particularly narrow. The same beam on a tower several hundred feet in the air on a windy day may seem very narrow.

RAIL CHARACTERISTICS

1. *Strength.* Rail strength applies to both the rail material and the rail supports. A rail may crumble under your weight if the supports are rotted or the foundation is not stable.

2. *Stability.* The term "fixed rail" implies an object that does not move, which is exactly what most rail walkers prefer. However, sometimes a rail will move a small amount. This is particularly true of fences and handrails that are not built for lateral stress. It is also true of rails made of semi-elastic materials (such as wood or steel) and having few vertical supports. Movement may indicate that a rail is not strong enough to hold you. Rails that move offer additional challenge for those who dare.

3. *Surface.* Balancing on a thin rail is difficult enough without having to worry about slipping off. Friction is a key to maintaining control. It's easier to walk on an old rusted railroad track than on one that has trains traveling on it daily. Add a little grease and wet sneakers on a rainy day and staying on a railroad track can test anyone's skills. I personally fell off a flat, two-lane-wide sidewalk once when the ice got the better of me.

4. *Size.* Width of the rail is obviously a key factor in determining how challenging a rail walk will be. Length, on the other hand, mostly enhances the walk. It is nice when you can get on a rail and go for a while.

5. *Site.* The location of a fixed rail has little to do with how technically challenging it is to walk, but it can be a major component of how adventurous it is to walk. Objective dangers such as long falls, falls into bodies of water, and falls into forbidden places that are hard to get out of would certainly intensify any fixed-rail walk.

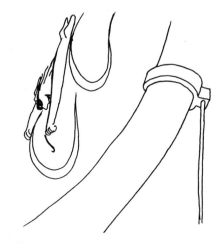

Single Points

Single-point balancing is the game of standing on the top of fire plugs, posts, poles, and parking meters. It is amazing how difficult just standing in one place can be, especially when the point is jiggling.

Technique

The basic techniques used to walk on slack chains and fixed rails are similar to the balance techniques used by downhill skiers, nordic racers, telemarkers, and dancers. Center your weight over your feet. Bend your knees to lower your center of gravity and keep your legs loose to make instant balance adjustments. Align your upper body by straightening your back and keeping your head up. And, in general, don't look at your feet; instead, *spot.*

Spotting

Spotting simply means keeping your eyes, and attention, focused on an object or place. Dancers spot to keep their balance when they spin and leap across a stage. Downhill skiers and telemarkers keep their balance by spotting, or looking, straight down the fall line. Chain walkers try to spot an object or discoloration (spot) on the anchoring wall or pole directly above the chain about eye height.

On a fixed rail, there may be nothing to spot except the rail itself. For example, the only other thing above the rail in the correct direction may be a tree moving in the wind. Your best body alignment for balance requires that you keep your head up, so pick a spot far down the rail. Try to

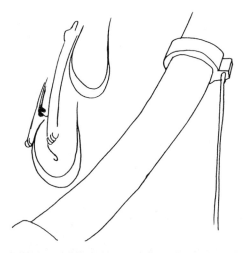

keep your spot at least twenty feet in front of you. As you move closer to your spot, pick a new spot further down the rail.

On a single-point balance, find any point in the direction you are facing and focus on it. A blur about eye level on the horizon is fine. Just keep your head up and don't look at your feet.

The key to balance is to keep your eyes on your spot.

Walking on Slack Chains

Few things look harder to do than walking on a slack chain. However, the skill is not that hard to learn. It just takes practice.

STARTING

1. Find a well-anchored chain made of strong steel medium-weight links. The chain should be close to the ground but should not touch the ground when your weight is on it.

2. Stand beside the chain near the center. The center is the most controllable part of the chain. Do not stand on the exact center because there is often a change in the chain's dynamics right at the midpoint. Face the end of the chain that is furthest away from you and have your back to the end that is closest.

3. Place one foot lengthwise on the chain. You should feel that the chain is centered under your foot. It should run under the center of your heel, just to the side of the ball of your foot and between the second and third toes.

4. Pick your spot on the wall or pole directly above the chain. If the chain is anchored at the top of a pole, you can spot the anchor point. (An anchor-point spot is not very good if you are close to the anchor and must tilt your head down to spot it.)

5. Step up on the chain. This should be done as smoothly as possible, but a little bit of a jump won't hurt. You want to have your weight directly over the chain. You do not want to cause the chain to move off to the side as you get on it. The chain will appear too wobbly before you attempt this. But once you step up on the chain, it will become much more stable. Keep your knee bent. Extend your arms for balance.

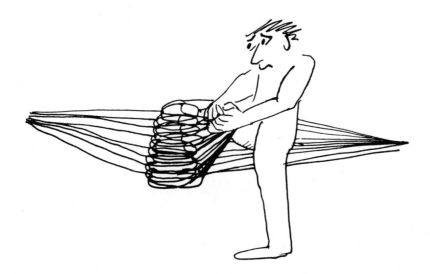

You can expect to fall off immediately the first few times that you try this. However, you will soon discover that it *is* possible for you to stand on a slack chain.

STAYING IN BALANCE

1. Keep spotting.

2. Stay low and loose. Bend your leg and keep it flexible. Don't lock your knee. This will allow you to absorb the chain's movement.

3. Extend your arms, but relax your shoulders. Extending your arms increases your stability. Changing your arm position can help adjust the center of your body mass and keep the center of your mass over the chain's at-rest position.

4. Relax your upper torso. A straight upper body need not be rigid. Think of your body as being aligned like a stack of blocks. No effort is required to keep them in place.

5. Breathe easy. Take long, even, deep breaths. Do not hold your breath. Your blood will flow. Your breath will flow. Remember, this is supposed to be relaxing.

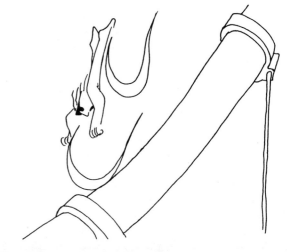

6. Ride the chain; don't fight it. If the chain swings, go with it like a surfer on a wave. Like a pendulum, the chain will always return to center. Guide it back and gradually dampen the chain's movement. Pushing down or bouncing on the chain can also bring it back to center.

7. Adjust your leg position as necessary. There are two schools of thought on the best leg position for balance: one advocates using the "one-leg technique," and the other recommends the "two-leg technique."

   a. Advocates of the one-leg technique claim that the best way to balance on a chain is by keeping one leg on the chain and letting the second leg hang freely. This allows the second leg to be used as a counterbalance for weight adjustments. Changing the distance between the second leg and the first leg changes the center of mass in the body. This technique is preferred by circus performers because it allows them to control balance without using their arms. This technique frees the arms for juggling and the like.

   b. Advocates of the two-leg technique claim that the best way to balance on a chain is to keep both feet on the chain. Once the second foot is on the chain, you can transfer your weight between your back foot and your front. You will notice that the chain moves away from the foot that is applying weight. By shifting your weight between feet you can make balance adjustments.

I personally use a combination of both techniques, applying whichever one suits my mood and the mood of the chain I am walking.

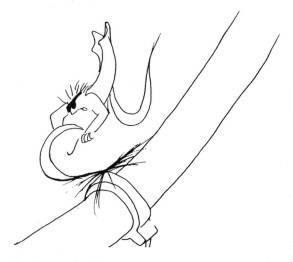

Falling Off

You can expect to fall off chains often, especially while learning, so plan your landing before you step up. Falling is part of the game. Actually, most falls amount to little more than stepping off the chain at the last second, which is easy to do and far better than actually taking an unexpected tumble. On the rare occasions when you can't stay on your feet, follow through by rolling gently off to the side, protecting your head and neck. Since most chain walking is done close to the ground, you will have to be very careless and/or unlucky to get hurt seriously.

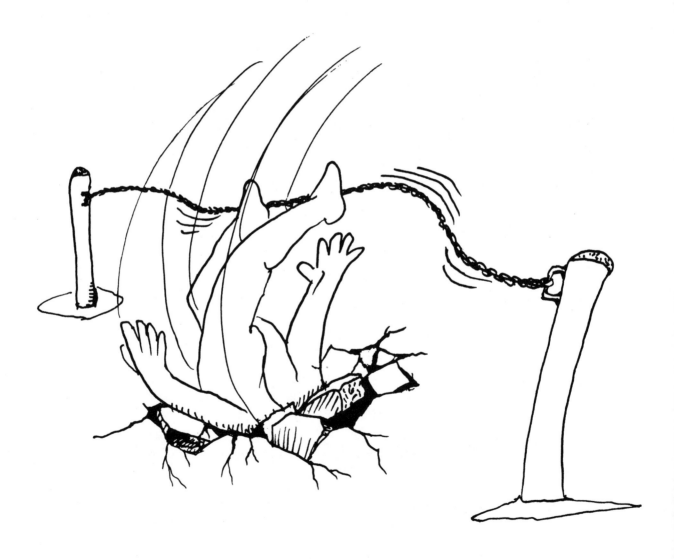

Walking Forward on a Slack Chain

1. Start from a balanced position, with your eyes focused on your spot. All of your weight should be on one foot. Your knee should be bent, with your leg flexible. The chain should be stable.

2. Prepare to make a small step. Bring your second foot toward the chain. Place it inches in front of your first foot. Feel for the chain. *Don't look at your feet; watch your spot.* Place your foot on the chain so that the chain runs down the center of your foot and not off to the side. If necessary, remove the foot and place it again until it is in the correct position. Keep your legs bent and flexible.

3. Slowly transfer your weight to the front foot. Find the new balance as you make the weight transfer. Maintain your spot and flexibility.

4. With all of your weight on the front foot, find a balanced position. Balance must be reestablished after each step.

5. When you are in balance, step again.

Walking Backward on a Slack Chain

Walking backward on a slack chain is essentially the same as walking forward. Balance must be established before executing each step. Maintain the same spot as if you were walking forward. When you are placing the foot behind you for backward motion, find the chain with your toe. Roll your foot down the chain from ball to heel to center the chain below your foot.

How To Turn

Turns are easiest when made three-quarters of the way across the chain. You want to be facing the upside of the chain, the end closest to you. It is best to have an idea where the new spot will be before turning.

1. Set or slide your front foot out so that there is a separation between the feet.

2. Put all weight on the front foot. Leave your back foot in contact with the chain.

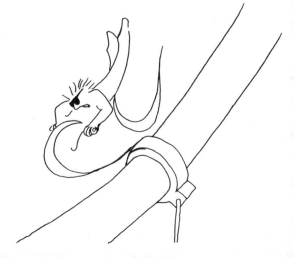

3. Swivel your hips around toward the new direction while maintaining your spot. This puts your hips parallel to the chain rather than in their usual perpendicular orientation. As you do this, rotate your back foot out so that the chain is running lengthwise under the ball of your foot, toes pointed in the new direction.

4. Turn your head and body toward the new spot on the opposite wall or pole. As you are turning, adjust your new front foot on the chain, then shift your weight to it. As you unweight, or push off, the new back foot, you can allow it to rotate.

5. Place all of your weight on the new front foot. Focus on the new spot and reestablish your balance.

Starting and Ending at a Post

Walking at the ends of a chain is tricky. As you swing back and forth, the waves you create on either side of you have different dynamics. On the side closest to the nearest anchor, the chain wants to swing with short, rapid movements. On the side furthest from the nearest anchor, the chain wants to swing with large, slow waves. As you are trying to ride the short, quick movements, the echo of the large, slow waves can sneak up and knock you off, especially if you are on a long, heavy chain.

One solution is to take advantage of your maximum stride when moving from a chain to a post or visa versa.

MOUNTING A POST FROM A CHAIN

1. Walk toward the post until you are as far from the post as you can be and still reach it with one more long step.

2. Step onto the post. The ball of your foot should be over the center of the post or on the place you want to balance. Your knee will probably be bent so that you are virtually squatting on that foot.

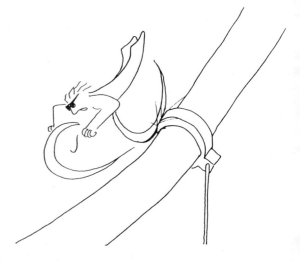

3. Transfer all of your weight to the foot on the post. Relax the other leg. Bring it in toward the post.

4. If this is the end post, stand up or step down off of the post. If you are continuing to walk on the chain, maintain this squatting position.

DISMOUNTING A POST ONTO A CHAIN

1. Squat down as low as possible while balanced on one foot and let the other foot hang free.

2. Place your free foot on the chain and apply weight to the foot on the chain while maintaining your balance on the post. This is to attract all of the slack in the chain that might have gathered in other segments.

3. Slide the free foot out on the chain as far from you as possible.

4. Gradually apply weight to the chain, establish your balance, and continue forward.

Walking on Fixed Rails

Walking fixed rails requires many of the same techniques as walking a slack chain. Bend the knees, extend the arms, keep your back straight, and spot. The major difference is that on chains you can adjust your balance by moving your body or moving the chain. On fixed rails you can only make balance adjustments by shifting your body position. On a fixed rail you must keep the center of your mass directly over the rail at all times.

Spotting may be complex on a fixed rail. Sometimes rails turn or are discontinuous. At these times you will have to look where you are going, but avoid looking at your feet unnecessarily. Return to your spotting as soon as possible even if the spot is just further along the rail.

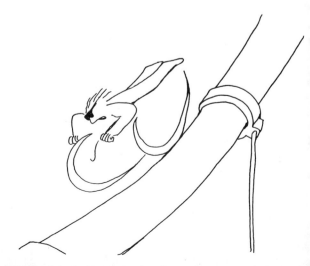

Standing on a Single-Point Balance

Many single-point balance problems are either just off the ground (for example, on parking meters or fire plugs) or easy to climb high enough to get your hands on top of (as on stop signs). The difficulty of standing on a single-point balance is directly related to how small of an area you are trying to stand on.

Three rules apply to every single point balance problem.

1. You want to get the ball of your supporting foot centered over the point you are trying to stand on.

2. Use your second foot to help you balance while you are trying to get in position by holding it against the object you are trying to stand on.

3. Keep your hands out of the way. If you need your hands, place them on holds that do not interfere with your supporting foot's placement.

If possible, place your second foot on a lower hold from which you can step directly onto the place you want to balance. For example, you can step on the bolts holding a sign prior to stepping onto the top of the sign post.

If there is no way to step or jump to your one-point stance, you may have to shimmy up the pole and use the manteling technique at the top (see "Buildering," page 17). Place your hands on top of the pole. Pull your weight up so that the top of the pole is chest high, then push down so that the top of the pole is at your waist. Hold yourself there with one hand, using as little of the top of the pole as possible, and place your opposite foot on the rest of the top of the pole. Gradually remove your hand and slide your foot so that the ball of your foot is centered on the top of the pole. Try not to step on your own fingers in the process (which I have done more than once). Stand up using your other foot braced against the pole for balance.

Safety and Special Risks

1. Before you mount a chain, cable, fixed rail, or single-point balance, make sure that the entire system is capable of holding all of the stress you will place on it.

2. Make sure chain links are not held together with a bad hook or piece of wire. Gradually sitting and swinging on a chain is a good way to test it. When you first step up on a chain or cable, keep your mouth closed. If it suddenly breaks, you won't want your teeth crashing against each other or your tongue when you hit the ground.

3. Never walk a thin cable near or above groin height without a well-defined front-to-back tread pattern on your shoes. A thin cable will tend to roll or slip from underfoot. It will then snap back like a bow string to its equilibrium position, which can be painful.

4. When walking on fences, don't fall on the dog's side.

5. Make sure the top of your single-point balance object is well attached and won't break off from under your foot.

Etiquette

- Don't touch the chain when someone else is on it. It is fun to make someone else slip off, but that person will only get you back worse later.

- Chain walking tends to attract gawkers. It is OK to ignore them, but try to abstain from offensive behavior when they are around.

- If you are going to bend a pole or destroy a chain by walking on it, don't walk on it.

- There are often good chains around car lots. Don't fall off and scratch the paint on any car, especially if it is new, for sale, clean, or if its owner is present.

- It is fine to ignore security guards who tell you to get down, because you are supposed to be concentrating and obviously cannot hear them. However, when one comes right up to you and screams in your face, politely step down, claim ignorance, promise anything, and leave rapidly.

Equipment

No special equipment is needed for slack chain, cable, or fixed rail walking, or for single-point balancing.

Clothing

Whatever you have on is OK as long as you can move in it.

Shoes

Anything that has a soft sole and will let you feel the chain cable or rail is good. Hard-sole shoes also work but they tend to be a bit slippery. Some people prefer ballet slippers. Some people prefer sneakers.

Hats

Hats are often worn by people who make a career of walking chains, cables, and the like. A hat can be held in the hand to make it look as if you are using it for balance. It can be placed on your head to make you look important. It can also be placed top-down in front of the chain if you are trying to attract spare change.

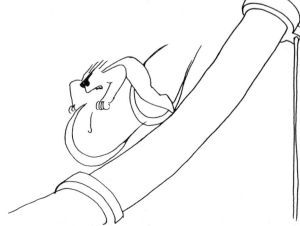

Spencer's Walk Above the Beach

I always thought of Spencer as a reasonable and sane kind of guy. We worked together word processing downtown. Sometimes after work we would go and get a couple of beers at the Scupper. There is nothing special about the Scupper's beer, but it has a great Happy Hour spread. You can scarf down all of the greasy chicken wings and potato chips you want for the price of a beer and call it dinner.

We would usually have a beer or two, eat too many chicken wings and chips and walk over to the bank parking lot around the corner. There was a chain across the parking lot after hours that we liked to walk on.

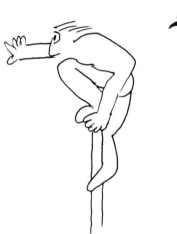

Spencer always told me that the key to walking on a slack chain is to clear your mind and focus on one spot until you get there. He would hop on the chain, and walk forward and backward. He would do turns and every once in a while try a new trick. I was always impressed. On good days I could almost make the length of the chain, but I could never turn. Too much greasy chicken and beer, I guess.

One Saturday, Spencer called me up to see if I wanted to go to the beach. It was a beautiful sunny and windy day. I said yes.

Spencer was really bummed out when I saw him. His shoulders sagged and he had grey mist in his eyes. His girlfriend had just left for Chicago. Some kind of career opportunity or something, he said.

We started talking and walking along the cliffs. We came to a place where thirty feet of cliff had fallen into the sea. There was an old rusty cable that spanned the gap and disappeared into the cliff on both sides. It was one inch in diameter on the part that hadn't unraveled and about three-quarters of an inch in diameter on the part that had. A hundred feet below, the waves crashed against rocks.

I couldn't believe it when Spencer stepped onto that cable. He applied his weight without knowing if the ends were secure. He didn't seem concerned. The cable shook.

The shock wave went across the span and echoed back. Spencer stood with one foot on the cable, the other in space. The rusty cable started to twist and unravel, then stopped. The water below crashed on the rocks. The wind had stopped.

His steps were tentative but firm. The cable swayed a little and twisted a bit. You could hear the crackle and creak of rusted metal as he stepped.

He reached center. Two feet away, where the cable changed thicknesses, the metal exterior strands were slowly unraveling toward him. A big gust of wind came up carrying the roar of the ocean. He turned and dove toward the cliff. I have never seen a person jump so far. He landed, arms extended, belly first on the cliff, with his legs dangling over the edge.

I ran to help him. He stood up. I could see the blood pumping through his neck. All the fire of life had returned to his eyes. He had regained balance.

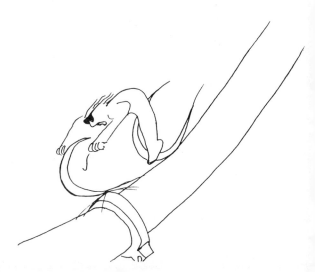

URBAN ADVENTURE
BIKE RIDING

"Beware of things with a small brain-to-body mass ratio . . . like cars."
BODIVOODOO

Streets are the arteries of urban life. They are rivers that carry goods and people from island to island. They are also raging torrents filled with roaring monsters. Tons of bent, misshapen, jagged-edged metal monsters coughing noxious gasses propel themselves at tremendous velocities down narrow corridors. Most people dare not enter these rivers without strapping themselves into a suit of armor, which itself is the beast in someone else's nightmare.

Once inside their two-ton, fully automatic, air-conditioned, stereo equipped, metal jackets, the drivers of the monsters feel safe. Their world seems orderly. Everyone goes in straight lines in the same direction. They think about work. They adjust their hair in the mirrors. They look for tapes in the glove compartments. They sip on their beers. They get lost in their fantasies. They do this every day. They are on automatic pilot. They expect no surprises.

The surge of monsters speeds up, slows down, and screeches to a halt. Paint is scraped, metal is bent, bones are crushed, people die. In fifteen minutes, traffic is back to normal. Only the smallest fragment of headlamp glass wedged between two pebbles in the pavement marks the spot. It is a hostile environment for soft-flesh creatures.

This is a perfect playground for the **URBAN ADVENTURER.** On a bicycle, the **URBAN ADVENTURER** can dance in the traffic like a kayaker picking his way through a rock garden in the middle of a white-water rapid. A bicycle is light, fast, and maneuverable. The speed and thrill of bike riding in traffic is directly

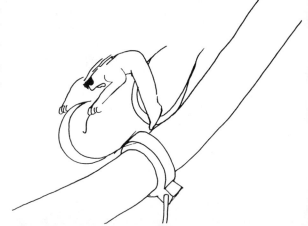

79

proportional to the amount of energy you have to put into it. The more you are bursting with energy, the faster you can ride. The degree of thrill and the corresponding dose of adrenalin is within your direct control.

URBAN ADVENTURE bike riding is not the same as bike touring through cities or using a bike as transportation in an urban environment. Bike tourists and commuters generally try to minimize their contact with traffic. This makes good sense. Traffic is dangerous and auto exhaust is sickening. Furthermore, the objectives of tourists and commuters are sight-seeing and transportation. When the **URBAN ADVENTURER** rides, he may have a destination and he may enjoy the scenery, but he defiantly seeks out traffic and rides for the thrill.

The skills described in this chapter are applicable for any type of bike riding in an urban environment. Tourists and commuters use many of the same techniques to increase their margins of safety. However, the **URBAN ADVENTURER** uses these techniques to assess the margin of safety so that he can then move further into the margin and come closer to the edge.

Many of the techniques described in this handbook are also used by skateboarders who ride in traffic in a similar manner as bicyclists. Hills are required for skateboarders to reach and maintain traffic speeds. Few adults have the necessary combination of skill, courage, concentration, and belief in immortality to participate in this activity successfully.

The Medium

The best place to do adventurous urban riding is on streets in commercial districts. Commercial streets tend to have a lot of traffic. Traffic flows at speeds attainable on a bicycle. Cars, trucks, and busses exhibit random motion. You never know what to expect as vehicles change lanes, make right and left turns, back up for parking, accelerate through red lights, make U-turns, and suddenly stop in the middle of the road to get quick cash from an automatic teller machine.

There are three different types of commercial districts preferred by **URBAN ADVENTURE** riders.

Neighborhood Shopping Areas

Neighborhood shopping areas offer interesting, challenging, and fun urban riding. There are usually two lanes of traffic, one in each direction. All streets feeding into the main commercial street have stop signs or traffic lights. The main commercial street itself has occasional stop signs and traffic lights. Cars line the streets. They are parked at meters, in loading zones, in bus stop zones, or in front of fire hydrants and driveways, and double parked everywhere. Traffic conditions depend on the time of day. Vehicles seldom go over 25 miles per hour. Average speed is between 10 and 15 miles per hour. Occasionally, the streets are so clogged with vehicles that it appears as if it would be faster to walk.

For the urban rider this scene is heaven. When traffic flows, you pace it. A souped-up Mustang's half-block lead on a three-block interval is soon lost as you whiz through the stop sign and gain a full block on the competitor. When traffic slows, you race it. It becomes a slalom course. You weave your way around one car on the right and another on the left, dodging fenders and jaywalkers, trying not to end up sprawled out on the hood of an Oldsmobile.

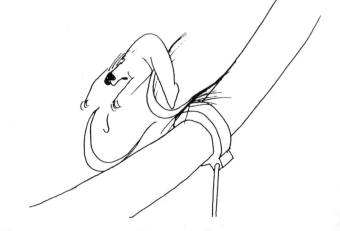

Unfortunately, most neighborhood shopping areas are only a few blocks long. However, if you connect them, you can get in a lot of good riding.

Avenues of Commerce

Avenues of commerce typically have four lanes of traffic, two in each direction. Parked cars line the streets. Traffic lights are common at all major intersections. The speed limit is usually under 35 miles per hour. Traffic flows at between 25 and 35 miles per hour.

When traffic is flowing, the urban rider has to be moving fast to enjoy avenues of commerce. This is best accomplished by drafting other vehicles, or riding directly behind them. Traffic lights are usually timed, which allows you to get momentum and keep it.

Drivers are often bothered when they notice you riding so close to their back bumpers. They often speed up to shake you. Of course, they generally can't go far before they are tailgating the vehicle ahead of them. When they touch their brakes, you can swerve out to ride on the broken line between the lanes. If the traffic flow is steady, you can drop back in behind the same vehicle again or pick another. If traffic starts to slow because a light has turned red, you can stay on the broken line and coast on up to the front of the pack. If the traffic flow speeds up to a pace you cannot maintain, you can look for an opening between vehicles and swerve back to the right.

When traffic is particularly heavy or when the lights are not timed properly, avenues of commerce are much like neighborhood commercial districts. One difference is that traffic on avenues of commerce moves faster. Another difference is that multiple lanes allow you to do more maneuvering in and among vehicles.

Downtowns

Downtown areas are ideally suited for urban riding. At the bottom of the dark, human-made canyons traffic flows in fits and starts. Streets are often one-way and almost always choked with vehicles. You can dodge between trucks and race taxicabs. The riding in downtown areas requires extensive maneuvering and lane changing. These areas are breeding grounds for bike messengers, couriers who make their living darting in and out of teeming downtown traffic.

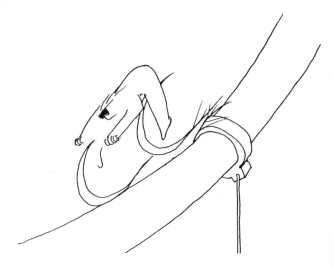

Technique

As a bike rider in a sea of cars, you are the most vulnerable person on the road. If you have a collision with an automobile, you will lose. Therefore, it is imperative that you avoid contact with cars at all times. If you do make physical contact with a car, it will not matter whose fault it is. Your bicycle and body will pay the largest price. The car will suffer minor damage at most and the driver will be physically unscathed.

The best ways to avoid collisions are to: (1) make sure that you see all vehicles in your vicinity, (2) make sure that you are seen by all drivers in your vicinity, (3) anticipate the movement of all vehicles and be out of their way (never expect a vehicle to slow or stop for you), and (4) know your stopping zone. Stopping zone is the distance required for you to stop. If a stationary vehicle or other object is in the stopping zone, you must maneuver around it or you will hit it.

The techniques described in this chapter are for the person who is already a proficient bicycle rider. If you are not, you have no business riding in traffic. Learn how to ride on a quiet country road or a residential suburban street. Advance to long tours, rides on wide roads with wide shoulders, and outings on city streets with bike lanes. After you are completely comfortable on your bicycle, when your bicycle is an extension of your body and riding in traffic becomes routine, you will be ready to think about **URBAN ADVENTURE** riding.

Where To Look

As you speed into danger, your survival will depend on your ability to identify hazards in sufficient time to avoid them. Keep your eyes moving. Use your peripheral vision to keep a wide-angle view of the greater situation. Monitor what is going on behind you by listening and periodically looking over your shoulder. Prioritize potential hazards immediately. Focus your attention on immediate threats first, upcoming threats second, and anything else last. For example, be aware that your quick turn to avoid a beer truck may send you rolling into an open manhole.

In general:

1. *Look far ahead.* On a bicycle you can see above most cars. You can also ride the line between lanes, which usually offers long sight lines. Know what you are going to encounter before you get there. Anticipate vehicle and road hazards that will be in your stopping zone. Respond to traffic conditions before the vehicles immediately ahead of you.

2. *Monitor the movement of everything beside you,* especially vehicles. Anticipate vehicles that enter from parallel lanes, side streets, driveways, and parking lots. Continually plan evasive action should a vehicle shift into your lane. Devise contingency plans as the situation changes.

3. *Stay attentive to the dangers approaching from behind you.* Listen for vehicles and glance over your shoulder to evaluate your margin of safety. Traffic behind you is the most dangerous. You are in its path and you cannot see it to get out of the way.

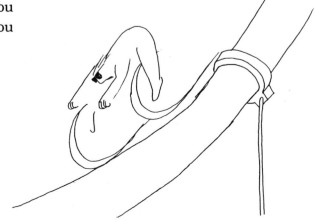

Riding Along Parked Vehicles

Riding along a line of parked vehicles requires focus beyond the general requirements, especially when you are boxed in by fast-moving traffic on the other side. You must be prepared for vehicles pulling out of their parking spaces, vehicle doors opening, and pedestrians emerging from between vehicles. There is often little room to maneuver. As you reduce your margin of safety by increasing your speed, keen awareness becomes more vital.

1. *Watch for motion.* A vehicle or person in motion is detectable even if you are not looking in that exact direction. Vehicles and people in motion are more likely to enter your stopping zone than those that are stationary. If they are in motion, it is likely that they have not seen you. This makes them threatening.

2. *Flashing turn signals* are a sign that the driver intends to enter your lane. He may or may not see you before proceeding.

3. *Turned wheels* signal potential danger. Only vehicles with wheels turned toward the lane can enter it.

4. *Check for a person in the driver's seat by looking through the back window.* If the seat is occupied, that person may either open a door or attempt to pull the vehicle into your path.

5. *Look at rearview mirrors.* The mirror on the side of a vehicle will often show the reflection of a driver's face. This is another indication of a person intending to pull into your path or exit a vehicle. You can also see if the driver is looking before proceeding.

6. *Look and listen* for other signs that the vehicle is about to move, such as a blast of exhaust emerging from the tail pipe or the sound of a vehicle being put into gear.

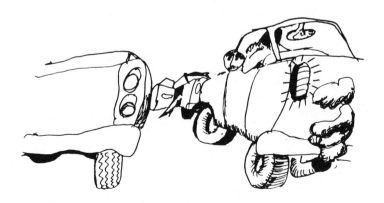

Riding the Center Line

Riding down the center of a road, between opposing directions of traffic, is like piloting a high-speed low-flying jet. Things happen fast, there is little room for error, and mistakes can be fatal. You must be aware of oncoming vehicles as well as those moving in your direction. This position is often used in neighborhood shopping areas when traffic is moving slowly or has completely stopped. Pay special attention to:

1. oncoming traffic. Be aware of drivers moving erratically or hugging the edge of the center line;

2. extra wide loads coming in your direction;

3. oncoming vehicles passing another stopped vehicle in their own lane by coming into the oncoming lane (your lane). This is very typical in congested traffic; and

4. vehicles in your own direction pulling out to pass a stopped vehicle in your own direction. Often the driver will not even look to see if he himself is being passed. The driver typically just focuses on his own frustration with traffic and the clearing that he sees in the oncoming lane. Watch for vehicle motion, signaling, and turned wheels as signs of this danger.

Position on the Road

The place you ride on the road is primarily a function of your speed in relation to the speed of traffic. In general, if you are riding slowly you should ride on the right shoulder if possible. In urban environments, the right shoulder is usually occupied by parked cars. When there is a lull in traffic, ride just to the right of the center of the right lane. This puts you out of the reach of opening car doors and gives you a good view of the road ahead. When traffic picks up, ride next to the parked cars. This should leave plenty of room for traffic to get around you. There is always a danger of someone opening a car door or pulling out of a parking space. However, because you are moving slowly, you should have time to respond.

As you increase your speed, move to the left, into the right lane. This will give you more time to respond to unexpected movement of parked cars. Moving left allows you to see further down the line of parked cars. It also decreases the distance you will have to swerve if you need to avoid a hazard, such as a car door opening.

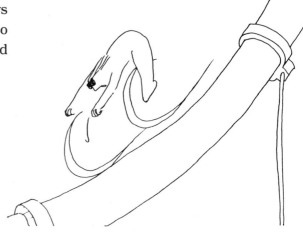

Moving to the left as you go faster does not make you more vulnerable from behind. On the contrary, since you are further in the road you are more visible and the drivers behind you should see you sooner. Also, as you go faster, the relative speed between you and a vehicle approaching from behind decreases. The driver not only sees you sooner but has more time to respond.

By the time you are moving at the speed of traffic, you should take your rightful place, slightly left of the center of your lane. The actual center of the lane generally has the most dripped oil on it, which can make it slippery. Also, more debris tends to collect in the center of a lane than closer to the areas where the auto tires roll.

When you are moving faster than right lane traffic, pass on the left. Look over your shoulder before changing lanes to make sure it is safe. If you can maintain the speed of left lane traffic, stay there. If you cannot, or if there is only one lane in each direction, return to the right lane after you have passed the slower vehicle.

Riding in the Spaces Between Parked Cars

In general, it is better to hold your position in a lane than to move over on the shoulder between parked cars. However, sliding in between parked cars can be useful if you are moving slower than traffic, the lane is narrow, there is a wave of traffic about to pass you, and there is a large gap in the line of parked cars. Don't move too far to the right. The ideal position is just inside the outer edge of the line of parked cars. This position offers some protection from behind the parked cars. It is also close enough to the traffic lane for you to be seen. If you go too far into the protected area between parked cars, you will not be seen by traffic. You want to give drivers time to see you before you reenter the lane when you need to pass the upcoming parked vehicles. If there is only a small space between parked cars, it is usually not worth changing position. It is better to stay more visible. The exception is if a large truck is passing and you want to give it ample room.

The spaces between parked cars are also useful if you want to speed past cars on the right when the road is narrow. This maneuver takes split-second timing if traffic is moving and is definitely a shortcut to high-stakes adventure.

Finally, the spaces between parked cars offer curb access for those riders who alternate between sidewalk and road riding. The spaces make good on-ramps, allowing you to pick up speed before reentering the lane.

Riding on Sidewalks

URBAN ADVENTURE riding is not confined to the streets. Some riders enjoy taking their bikes on the sidewalks, weaving around pedestrians, narrowly missing stationary objects, and darting back into traffic. In general, I advise against riding on sidewalks as part of **URBAN ADVENTURE** rides because the ride is slower and because it shifts the danger from you to unwary pedestrians. The exception is when there is good reason to get off the street and no pedestrians are on the sidewalk.

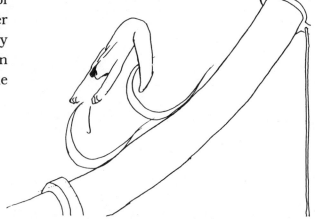

Hopping Curbs

Hopping curbs gives you access to sidewalks, allows you to cross many road center dividers, and is just plain fun. It increases your mobility, expands your riding terrain, allows you to take advantage of shortcuts, and can get you out of the way of danger—fast.

Hopping a curb is just like popping a wheely except that the wheely is only held for a second and then you immediately unweight the back wheel.
To learn to hop curbs, find a nice, quiet, trafficless street with a curb no more than four inches high.

A. *Practice popping wheelies while rolling slowly.*

1. Start with your lead foot just past the top of the pedaling cycle. (Your lead foot is the one that you would put forward if you were lining up for a sprint or about to make a jump.)

2. Push down with your lead foot and at the same time pull up on the handle bars by throwing or jerking your upper body backward. You want to get all of your weight back over the back wheel at once. This is counter intuitive and will take lots of practice. Be careful. When you finally get it right, you are likely to do it too hard and go over backward.

3. Do this several times until your wheely requires minimal effort and you can control the height you lift the front wheel off the ground.

B. *Practice lifting the back wheel up while rolling slowly.*

1. Start with your lead foot forward in the pedaling cycle.

2. Simultaneously a) throw your upper body weight forward over the front wheel, b) make a jumping motion that will raise your pelvis in the air while keeping your feet on the pedals, and c) grip the handlebars and roll them forward as though you were trying to rotate the bike end over end. It may help to think of a mule kicking.

3. Repeat these steps several times until you are comfortable lifting the back wheel.

C. *Practice lifting both wheels up at the same time.* This is the same as lifting the back wheel with a slight change in balance that you will easily find with practice.

D. *Practice alternating between lifting the front and back wheels.*

E. *Practice hopping up on curbs.*

1. Ride toward the curb slowly.

2. Pop a wheely to get your front wheel on the curb, then immediately,

3. lean forward to lift the back wheel up onto the curb.

Even though you probably won't be able to jump the back wheel up on the curb, you will be able to unweight the back wheel which will allow it to roll up on the curb on its own.

F. *Practice hopping off curbs.*

1. Ride to the edge of the curb.

2. As you are about to go off the edge, pop a wheely.

3. When you land on the street, try to land on your back wheel first.

After you learn the basics of curb hopping, it will be easy to apply the techniques to larger curbs when traffic is teeming and you are going fast. One difference is that you will want to lift both wheels in the air simultaneously to prevent rim damage if you are hopping up on a curb while moving fast. This jumping technique can also be used to avoid road hazards.

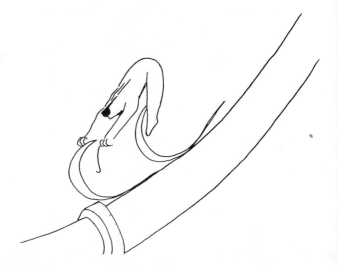

Drafting

Drafting is a term used by bicyclists to mean riding in the agitated air space directly behind another vehicle. The first vehicle encounters air resistance. As it  pushes the resistive air aside to let itself through, it creates a slight vacuum behind it. Previously displaced air rushes in to fill the vacuum. The air behind the vehicle is turbulent and generally moving in the direction of that vehicle. By riding behind another vehicle, a bicyclist can move at a greater speed because she does not encounter as much air resistance. Bike racers and tourists draft each other to save energy. Large surface areas are better to draft than small ones. It is easier to pedal behind a car than behind another bicycle. It is easier to pedal behind a truck or van than behind a car.

TO DRAFT:

1. While riding, move directly behind a vehicle. Position yourself so that you can look down the road in front of the lead vehicle. Directly behind the left fender is generally a good position.

2. Your front wheel should be as close to the lead vehicle as you are comfortable having it. Some riders keep within two inches of the lead vehicle. The closer you are, the better the drafting. A large truck will actually pull you along with it at high speeds if you are close enough.

3. Keep your eyes on the road ahead of the lead vehicle. Anticipate what the driver will react to. The disadvantage of being close is that you have very little reaction time. If a driver were to slam on the brakes unexpectedly, it would be difficult for you to avoid kissing the car's bumper. You want to know what the driver will do before he does it. Anticipate swerves. Anticipate braking.

4. If you start going too fast and are about to crash into the lead vehicle, swerve sideways just out from behind the vehicle. You will encounter wind resistance. Immediately swerve back or you will drop behind. While it is also possible to touch your brakes to slow down, the swerving method is preferable. If the vehicle is slowing, you may want to pass it. Obviously, pay attention to oncoming traffic.

5. If the lead vehicle starts to pull away, pedal faster. It is much easier to stay behind a vehicle than to catch one. Once you are out of the draft it is very difficult to reenter it because you will be required to fight wind resistance to catch up.

Intersections

Intersections are the most dangerous and thrilling part of the road. They should be approached with caution. Even when you have the right-of-way you are at risk. The Bodivoodoo expressed his opinion about traffic lights clearly when he said, *"Red or green, it's all the same. Play it that way and you won't get hurt."* A light or a sign is not a physical barrier. People run traffic control devices every day. Often the offender is not even aware of what he is doing.

Approach each intersection as a separate and distinct riding situation. Use your peripheral vision to get the big picture of all vehicle and pedestrian movement. Watch for signs of turning vehicles. Indications are (1) signal lights, (2) hand signals, (3) vehicles pulled over to the far right, likely to turn right, (4) vehicles pulled over to the far left or stopped in the middle of an intersection likely to turn left, and (5) front wheels turned in one direction or the other.

Plan your route based on what you see, not on what you usually do. This may mean stopping, continuing straight, turning, running red lights, switching sides of the street, jumping traffic barriers, dodging in and out of oncoming traffic, or moving into pedestrian land to step out of the game for a moment. Whatever action you take, make it a conscious decision.

Entering an Intersection When You Have the Right-of-Way

If traffic is flowing when you go through an intersection, it is generally best to maintain your position. However, there are caveats and exceptions.

If you are riding on the right of traffic, beware of vehicles turning right. Do not expect that the driver will see you. The right side of a vehicle typically has a large blind area. Signs of imminent danger include blinking turn signals, vehicles that are over in the right side of the right lane, and front wheels that are turned right.

If you are on the right side of the right lane and you see a vehicle that will be turning right, move around the vehicle on the left. Obviously, look to make sure it is safe to move left. Traffic behind you will have to stop or get around the turning vehicle too.

If you are in the left lane, beware of vehicles turning left. Pass the vehicle turning left on the right side. This will be no problem. There is almost always enough room on the right side of the left lane for a bicycle to fit around a vehicle.

Making Turns

During high speed and aggressive **URBAN ADVENTURE** rides, turns are often best executed in accordance with standard traffic laws. Right turns should be made from the right lane. Left turns are usually best made from the left side of a one-lane each-way road, from the left lane of a two-lane each-way road, from the specified left turning lane, or from the right boundary of a series of left turning lanes.

However, when you come to a red light, left turns can also be made by cutting to the other side of the street in the crosswalk in the green-light direction. From there you can wait for the light to change before crossing to the right lane, or you can ride on the left side of the road until you can cut over to the right. If you notice a police officer while in the middle of this maneuver, hop off your bike and temporarily join the pedestrian world.

Approaching an Intersection With a Line of Stopped Vehicles

As you approach an intersection with a line of stopped vehicles, you can pass the vehicles on either the right or the left side. The side you choose will depend on your initial road position, whether you intend to turn, and the positions of the vehicles in the line. You can weave your way in and out of the line of cars, changing sides of the lane or position in several lanes as much as you want. This type of maneuvering is potentially dangerous and very fun.

Keep the entire field in view and continually pick your best course. On a bicycle you have a good vantage to pick a line that will keep you from being boxed in. You want to avoid tight corridors where you are likely to run into protruding mirrors or scratch the paint on a new Mercedes.

Only a few feet between vehicles is needed for you to change sides of a vehicle line. However, whenever you cut in front of a waiting vehicle, first make eye contact with the driver. Then, if he runs you over, at least it will have been deliberate.

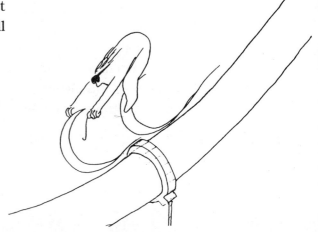

Running Stop Signs and Stop Lights

As a bicyclist you are subject to the same laws and responsibilities as other vehicle operators. This means that when you approach a stop sign, you are supposed to come to a full stop. If a police officer is present, it is best to put one foot on the ground. This action will indicate to the officer that you are no longer moving. Look both ways and proceed with caution when it is your turn.

Most bike riders do not stop at stop signs. **URBAN ADVENTURE** junkies seldom slow down. A degree of safety can be achieved by assessing the type of intersection, analyzing intersection dynamics, and seeking shielding when possible.

If you are positive that there are no vehicles that will hit you entering the intersection, you can run the light or sign safely. If you can clearly see that there are vehicles that will hit you, slow down and let them pass.

Not all vehicles that enter an intersection on a perpendicular course to your own are threatening. Some vehicles turn. Turning vehicles often provide a break in the traffic flow and allow you to run a light or sign. Other times there is enough space between vehicles to allow a fast-moving cyclist through. Judging the time/space opening between vehicles takes accurate depth perception and velocity analysis. As an **URBAN ADVENTURER** you will probably always want to cut it close to the edge. It is better to err on the conservative side. Always assume that drivers do not see you and will maintain their current speed or acceleration. If you estimate wrong, you can die.

Remember, if you are going to run a stop sign, you are betting on other vehicles not doing the same.

Running Stop Signs When Visibility Is Poor and Other Vehicles Are on a Course Parallel to Yours

This situation is common on urban rides in neighborhood districts. Ideally, you will want to time your crossing so that it coincides with a car going straight through the intersection in a direction parallel to yours. Rolling through an intersection concurrent with another vehicle has three advantages. First, you have the advantage of the driver's vision, assuming that the driver has already stopped and made sure the intersection was safe before proceeding. Second, the vehicle provides protection from one side if another driver on a perpendicular track runs a stop sign. Third, vehicles on a perpendicular track are less likely to enter the intersection if they see a vehicle already in it.

If you speed into a blind intersection, your mind must work fast to anticipate and assess all vehicle movement because you are trusting the eyes of an unknown driver. It is this type of split-second decision making that unnerves the timid, bolsters the bold, and feeds the wild animal inside every **URBAN ADVENTURER** yearning for excitement.

Momentum

It is easier to slip through a slot in traffic if you are already in motion than if you are starting from a stop. As you approach any intersection, maintain as much speed as possible, remembering that you may have to come to a complete stop at the crosswalk.

The momentum of motor vehicles is also important to remember. It is not difficult to run a fresh red light if all the perpendicular traffic is stopped and waiting to go. On the other hand, if the perpendicular traffic is moving and has anticipated an upcoming green light, running your red light could be fatal.

Ah yes, a standard four-way-stop intersection, complete with vehicle shielding. Now let's see . . .

Advantages of being on the right side:
- *I won't be next to oncoming traffic.*
- *I'll be protected from perpendicular traffic when I first enter the intersection.*
- *I'll be in a good position if the vehicle makes a left turn.*

Disadvantages of being on the right side:
- *I'll be in a dangerous position if the vehicle makes a right turn.*
- *I'll be close to parked cars.*
- *I'll be on the slow side of the road while moving faster than traffic.*

Advantages of being on the left side:
- *I'll be in the faster part of the road when I'm moving faster than traffic.*
- *I'll be away from parked cars.*
- *I'll be safer while in the second half of the intersection.*

Disadvantages of being on the left side:
- *I'll be more exposed to the perpendicular flow of traffic when I first enter the intersection.*
- *I'll be more at risk from oncoming vehicles.*
- *I'll be more at risk if the vehicle makes a left turn.*

Riding at Night

The technique for **URBAN ADVENTURE** riding at night is not much different than that used when riding during the day. A little more caution is needed to make sure that you are seen. Most urban riders use reflectors on bicycles and clothing.

Bike lights are the most effective means of illuminating a rider. A taillight is the most important. Flashing taillights work well. Front lights are not as necessary because street lamps and vehicle headlights generally provide enough light for you to see the streets. Being visible is the major issue. Being seen from behind is more important than being seen from the front. You can react to vehicles ahead of you and off to the side because you can see them. You cannot react as well to vehicles coming from behind. You have to depend on those drivers seeing you. Unfortunately, most vehicles coming close to you will be approaching from behind.
The safest way to ride at night is to assume that you are invisible and to make sure that you are out of the way of all vehicles.

Riding on Snow and Ice

URBAN ADVENTURE riding does not end in the winter for people who live in the colder parts of the world. In fact, it intensifies. Riding on snow and ice is more exhilarating and dangerous than riding on dry streets.

Riding on a little fresh snow is easier than most riders think. The back tire can get traction if it has some tread and weight on it while you are pedaling. The front tire acts like a ski. When you first turn, the front tire slips a bit. Snow builds up in front of the front tire because it is not parallel to the direction of motion. The snow buildup then pushes the front end of the bicycle over in the proper direction. It is just like riding on dry pavement, only the bicycle response time is a bit slower.

In deep, heavy snow, you have to ride on vehicle tire tracks. The packed snow makes a fine riding surface.

In very deep snow, no vehicles will be moving on the streets anyway. Break out the skis.

Traffic usually moves slower on snowy days. You will also find that you will ride slower. This is primarily because there is so much road resistance. One advantage of the slow traffic is that it gives everyone more time to react. That time is needed because roads are slippery and it is hard to stop.

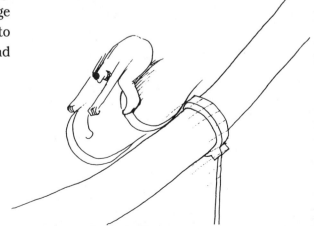

To stop a bicycle, it is best to ride off into the softer snow. It is easier to veer off than to actually stop. Brakes don't always work so well. The front brake is deadly; don't touch it or you might find yourself on the ground with cars slipping and sliding as they try to avoid running over you.

Riding on ice can be particularly treacherous. Turns and stops are difficult when there is an absence of friction between the tire and the road surface. Try to find an area of the road that is not smooth ice for these maneuvers. The smoothest ice is usually in the tire ruts. Often there is an apron of frozen snow outside the tire ruts. Stay on the frozen snow rather than on the smooth ice if there is a choice.

A few days past the last snowfall, the centers of the roads are often dry, making them good places to ride.

Safety and Special Risks

Most of the techniques described in this chapter are means of increasing your awareness of traffic as you proceed with an inherently dangerous activity. Following all traffic rules and yielding to all vehicles is the safest way to ride on city streets. Staying off narrow streets and those with heavy traffic will also increase your margin of safety. Since most safety issues are discussed in depth in other sections of the chapter, this section will only discuss issues not previously explored.

Pedestrians

Pedestrians are not always the brightest animals on the road. The smart ones stay on sidewalks, cross at crosswalks when the light is green, or jaywalk deftly. The rest wander about like cattle. When they suddenly realize they are in the path of a speeding bicycle, they behave like squirrels. First they go one way, then the other, back and forth, unable to make up their minds. At the last second they stop and, with horror on their faces, watch impending doom bear down upon them.

Give pedestrians the right-of-way in crosswalks. If they are not aware of you, warn them of your approach as soon as possible. Many will get out of the way if they hear a bell or a shouted warning. Try indicating which side you will pass on. For example, shout, "Passing on your left!" About half will move or look in the correct direction. Try to avoid crashing into them no matter what they do. This usually means you have to slow down.

Belligerent Drivers

Some drivers are unwilling to share the road with bicycles. They pass extremely close to you when they go by. They turn right in front of you. They sit right behind you and pound on their horns. When you encounter this, get out of the driver's way and let him pass. He has the right to pass as close to you as he wants. If he misjudges and hits you, he will probably be gone before you can untangle yourself from your bent bicycle frame, pick the gravel out of your face, and wipe away enough blood from your eyes to look for a licence plate number.

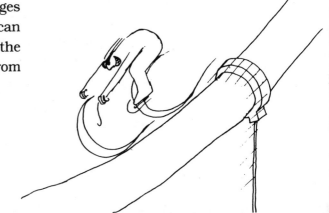

Extremely Narrow Streets

Extremely narrow streets or streets with narrow lanes can be problematic for the bike rider who is not moving at the speed of traffic. If you feel you have no alternative to being on the street, move closer to the center of the lane. As a bike rider, you have as much right as any other vehicle on most roads. It is better to be so much in the way that other vehicles will not even try to get around you. If the constricted corridor persists for a long distance, pull over when you can to let the backed-up traffic pass.

Road Hazards

There are many types of road hazards. Some can damage your body, others can damage your bike. Although it is important to avoid road hazards, it is also important not to be hit by a truck while avoiding them.

Glass and debris are usually found on the right side of the road. Try to notice early. Move into the right lane gradually. You want to avoid swerving into the center of a lane when there is traffic. Look over your left shoulder to see if it is safe before moving over. If it is not safe, or if you do not have time to check, take the flat tire.

Water drainage grates can be deadly. Sometimes the longitudinal holes are wide enough to catch a bicycle tire. If your front tire goes into one, it will stop your bike immediately and send you headfirst. Avoid the grates, particularly if the holes are parallel to your rolling direction. If one is impossible to avoid due to traffic, make sure your front wheel avoids the holes in the grate. Either roll over the metal parts or pop a wheely over the entire grate.

Railroad and streetcar tracks will also catch tires and dump bike riders. To avoid being caught in them, cross them as close to perpendicularly as possible. This may not be easy, particularly if tracks are running down the street and you are speeding along in traffic. In this case, cross the tracks by turning sharply across them with your front tire. Make sure the front tire crosses the tracks at a 45 degree angle or more. Don't worry as much about the back tire. Back tires seldom get caught in tracks, and if they do, you probably will not lose all control.

Grease, oil, diesel fuel, or gravel on the road surface makes the road slippery and hazardous while you are turning. Obviously, try to avoid these hazards. If you find yourself on a slippery surface, just roll through it and try to avoid applying your brakes, especially the front brake. If you apply your back brake and begin to slide, turn into the slide. If you apply your front brake, you will probably loose control of your steering and go down.

Debris such as paper bags and boxes blow around in the middle of the road. Restrain yourself and try not to run over them. They may contain bottles or some other object that can cause you to lose your balance, puncture your tire, or bend your rims.

Etiquette

Most drivers are respectful of bicyclists. They are perfectly willing to share the road. In return it is only fitting that the cyclist show respect to motor vehicles.

- When you are stopped at a light and a car in the right lane is waiting to make a right turn, get out of the vehicle's way so the driver can proceed. This is easily accomplished by moving to the left and letting the vehicle pass to the right around you. If the light turns in the process, you are in a good position to jump out ahead of right-lane traffic.

- When you are moving slowly, move way over to the right to let motor vehicles behind you pass. Give the vehicles lots of room. They will appreciate it, and you will reduce your chances of getting run over.

• It is also best not to alienate pedestrians. When you must pass close to pedestrians, slow down so you don't scare them. Pass behind pedestrians in crosswalks. They will be less likely to notice you and less likely to do something unpredictable.

• When you are riding on a sidewalk and scare a pedestrian, smile and be friendly. Saying, "Hello, nice day isn't it?" and apologizing are both acceptable.

Equipment

Any functioning bicycle will work. It can have one or more speeds and one or more brakes. Most important is that you enjoy riding it.

Some urban riders prefer bicycles with the traditional ten-speed road bike configuration. Some prefer mountain bikes. Some prefer upright one speeds or three speeds. The decision is usually based on what the rider can afford, what he is used to, and the particular topography and wind patterns in his riding environment. Certain characteristics are desirable for any bike. You want the bike to be lightweight, well lubricated, and tuned for proper performance.

Gears

Multigear bicycles are advantageous where there are a lot of hills and/or wind. The same gearing ranges are available on both road bikes and mountain bikes. Road bikes used to have ten "speeds." Now they typically have twelve, fifteen, eighteen, or twenty-one "speeds," although they still look like the same "ten speeds." Mechanical advantage is a function of gear ratios, and the same gearing can be added to any bike frame. Usually mountain bikes come in lower ranges, but mountain bikes and road bikes can both be customized to meet the user's needs.

In flat urban areas with little wind, a one-speed bike can be an excellent choice. It will tend to cost less and weigh less.

A good three-speed bike can be great for **URBAN ADVENTURE** riding. However, be careful: three-speed hubs are not designed for high stress and have been known to slip out of gear. This can be dangerous if it happens when you are standing up and cranking. Typically, the rider will slip off the pedal, straddle the upper bar on the bike frame, and wind up sliding along the pavement. This happened to me one enthusiastic morning after too much coffee.

Tires

There is a growing controversy about whether fat-tired mountain bikes or skinny-tired road bikes are better.

Fact: Narrow and lightweight tires offer less road resistance and rotational inertia than fat tires do.

This means the rider can accelerate faster and maintain a greater speed with less effort using skinny tires. Many riders claim that they can go as fast, or faster, on their mountain bikes than on their road bikes. One explanation could be that the overall quality and condition of the mountain bike is better than that of the road bike.

Fact: Fat tires and rims are better able to withstand the abuse of potholes and curbs than skinny tires and rims are.

Nothing the urban streets can offer requires the strength and durability of a good mountain bike wheel except high-speed curb jumping. Even if streets are particularly bad, a medium-weight touring tire and rim will be adequate.

Toe Clips

Toe clips are useful for two reasons. First, they allow the rider to direct more power to the wheels. This allows you to go faster. Second, using toe clips reduces knee injury related to strain. Pushing down on the pedals uses one set of muscles and pulling up uses another. The second set of muscles works in contrast to the first. When both sets are used, there is a balanced use of the knee joint.

Bike Geometry

Bike geometry is a matter of personal preference. Shorter wheel bases and steeper frame angles accelerate more rapidly and turn more quickly. Longer wheel bases and relaxed angles offer stability and a more comfortable ride, particularly on bad roads. Neither has a distinct advantage for **URBAN ADVENTURE** riding. Your choice depends on what you like and are used to.

Handlebar position is also a matter of personal preference. Lower bars bend the rider over and reduce air resistance. Higher bars allow the rider to be more upright and improve visibility.

Both styles are fine for **URBAN ADVENTURE** riding. However, bars that allow the rider an upright position are better for snow and ice riding.

Winter Bikes

Riding on snow and ice takes a heavy toll on a bicycle. Many riders use a separate bicycle for winter. Snow and ice riding is best done on a very upright bicycle. Fenders are highly recommended. Bikes with geometry similar to the old three speeds are perfect. You want to have your weight evenly distributed between the wheels. You do not want to be hunched over. You want to be up and in position for a quick exit if you dump your machine. If you use toe clips, keep them loose. Many riders prefer women's frames for snow riding because they are easy to get away from in an emergency.

Winter bicycles require much more maintenance than dry-weather road bikes. Salt on the road creates rust problems. In parts of the country where sand or cinder are used instead of salt, some salt is still added to the mixture. The chain must be oiled every two or three rides. Other parts, such as derailleurs, free wheels, brakes, and cables, also need frequent oiling.

Some people use mountain bikes as their winter machines. Mountain bikes work well because of the wider tires and strong braking systems. However, old medium-weight upright bicycles are also excellent for winter riding. Used ones can usually be found for ten to fifty dollars with fenders. Ten-speed–type road bikes with narrow tires are not recommended.

Brakes

Your brakes should be able to stop you on the steepest hill when they are wet. Old side-pull brakes won't do that. Some of the newer brakes, like cantilever brakes, will.

Helmets

These days most bike riders use helmets. They are made of light, dense foam and will protect the rider should the rider fall on his head. Actually, using a helmet is unnecessary unless you fall on your head. It won't do much good if you land on your arm.

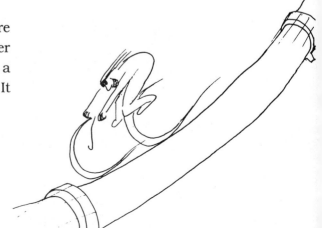

You have to make two mistakes before wearing a helmet is necessary. First, you have to come off of your bicycle. Second, you have to hit your head. It is easy to make the first mistake. Even good riders come off of their bikes occasionally. Making the second mistake depends a great deal on instinct. Some people naturally protect their heads and other people don't. If you decide not to wear a helmet and you make the first mistake, be real sure you don't make the second.

Eye Protection

Your eyes are very exposed when you are riding fast. Anything hanging in the air can hit you in the eyeball as you ride. Typically, these items include dust, insects, and gravel. You can protect your eyes by wearing sunglasses or any other form of eye protection.

Clothing

Pants should be flexible around the thighs and completely out of the way around the calves and ankles. Shorts or bicycling tights are best. Sweats are also good if you can keep them away from the chain. Avoid any pants or shorts that have a large seam through the crotch. They become very uncomfortable when you are on the seat for a long time.

Shirts or jerseys should be made of breathable, windbreaking material. Tight-fitting jerseys that won't flap in the wind are preferred by some riders. Just about anything comfortable will work well, including T-shirts, button-down oxford shirts, sweaters, and wind breakers. The best choices depends a lot on the weather. Light colors or reflective material are preferred for night riding.

Wear shoes, if you want.

Tandem

There was a punk rocker named Mike
who delivered the message by bike.
He rode around town,
ran pedestrians down,
a profession he really did like.

He then met a woman named Clair
who wore spikes all over her hair.
She rode a bike, too,
for something to do,
and was always up for a dare.

In traffic for hours they'd play.
It occupied most of their day.
Through stop signs they'd run;
the danger was fun
'Cause riding the edge was their way.

Once just for kicks that were random
they decided to hop on a tandem.
Through streets they did soar
creating uproar.
Cops chased but could no way land 'em.

Around cars and trucks they did race,
swerving all over the place,
escaping sure death
by just half a breath,
maintaining the rocket ship pace.

The adrenalin showed in their eyes.
They looked up to watch the moon rise.
With dripping sweat bands,
they stopped and touched hands,
then went on to eat two pizza pies.

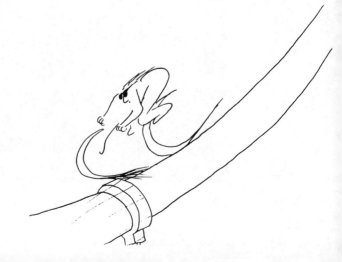

URBAN SPELUNKING

"Trust your intuition, not your fear."
BODIVOODOO

The world beneath the urban landscape lures a different type of **URBAN ADVENTURER** in search of a different type of terror. It is a world of claustrophobic caverns, disorienting darkness, and suffocating stench. The thrill of subterranean **URBAN ADVENTURE** is that of exploration. The focus of subterranean adventure is on the place rather than the activity. No special physical skills are needed to become proficient at subterranean **URBAN ADVENTURES.** For example, special balancing and body positioning techniques are not usually used. The excitement comes from uncovering hidden secrets while wandering the forbidden bowels of the urban environment.

The allure of walking dark passages is the allure of the unknown. The subterranean explorer acts out the archetypal journey into the underworld. There is the threat of becoming lost. There is the hope of finding treasure. There is the fear of being constricted or buried alive. There is the confrontation with real and imaginary danger. And there is the joy only experienced when you emerge from darkness into the fresh light of day.

The Medium

Man-made caverns are only built to serve specific functions. Generally, they are not designed for human presence. If human passage is possible it is either through maintenance access or because a particular conduit is not functioning to capacity. Typically, tunnels are sculptu-

111

rally monotonous, muddy or dusty, devoid of color, and, of course, dark. Yet, unexplainably, there is a lure that draws adventurers to seek the ends of each passageway.

Culverts

Culverts are the most common and easily accessible subterranean urban environments. Most children, would-be spelunkers, have explored culverts. These channels function to provide water passageways under roads during wet weather. When not flooded, they are good places to find insects, amphibians, reptiles, and assorted debris. The actual tunnel is generally made of corrugated metal or concrete pipe. Culverts tend to be short tunnels. Passage usually requires crawling.

Storm Drainage Systems

Storm drains remove unwanted liquid waste from the urban environment and prevent flooding. A storm drain system may or may not be connected to the sewage disposal system. Older urban areas tend to have combined sewage and storm systems. Modern urban areas tend to have separated systems.

If the storm drain system is not connected to the sewage system, it could be a great place to explore. Passage is generally easiest in dry conditions. Most underground piping in storm drain systems is too constricted for adult human passage. However, larger main conduits do exist. In Toronto, Canada, some avid spelunkers in search of an **URBAN ADVENTURE** found a network of five- and six-foot-high tunnels, which they explored on their mountain bikes.

Treasures abound in the underworld. Water from rain, snowmelt, garden overflows, car wash, and other sources picks up debris and flows into the storm drain inlet. Objects such as lost jewelry, old tires, and baby carriages have been known to travel through storm drain systems.

Storm drainage systems are likely habitats for rats and roaches. Rumor has it that alligators live under the streets of New York City.

There are a couple of ways to obtain access in a storm drain system. Perhaps the best is to enter through a drainage outlet. Large pipes that dump storm water are found along natural waterways, including rivers, lakes, bays, etc. Access is also possible through manholes above storm drain inlets.

Sewage Systems

The idea of sewer exploration conjures images of giant medieval stone passageways under cities like Paris, Rome, and Istanbul. But in most urban areas the reality of sewer exploration would be far less romantic. Older sewers are made of brick, and modern sewers are made of concrete. They may be cylindrically shaped, rectangular, or shaped like an inverted egg. They are designed for drainage and do not have walkways.

Operating sewer systems can be extremely dangerous. They contain the biological waste of the urban area. They are so filled with bacteria that most sewage repair work is done by remote control. When people are required to go down into a sewage system and maintain larger tunnels, they don full deep-sea-diver-like costumes, complete with oxygen tanks and expensive electronic gas monitoring devices.

Even when sewage tunnels are passable, they can be deadly. Bacteria can consume enough of the oxygen to make the air unable to support human life. Toxic gasses, such as carbon monoxide and hydrogen sulfide, form in sewer tunnels.

Underground Transit Tunnels

Many urban regions have underground transit systems. There is access in to the tunnels from both station platforms and train entry/exit ports. However, there is often some type of surveillance at the access and usually some type of minimal barrier that must be crossed.

I've never found much of general interest inside a transit tunnel except the thrill of being there. The excitement comes from making the passage and living to tell. Underground transportation vehicles are usually electric powered. There is either a third rail or wires overhead containing high voltage electricity used to power the vehicle. If the vehicles travel on rails, there are usually two sets of tracks, one for each direction. Sometimes there are walkways. There are usually periodic alcoves that can be ducked into if the subway vehicle is coming. And, of course, you can expect to see the ubiquitous graffiti.

General Public Utility Access Vaults and Tunnels

Beneath many manhole covers are vaults that provide access to underground public utility lines. Generally, each utility maintains its own vaults. The electric company, gas company, telephone company, cable TV company, etc. all have separate vaults. The vaults are generally rectangular concrete boxes. Conduits containing wires or pipes enter and exit the vaults from different sides.

It is rarely possible to obtain underground passage from one vault to the next. One exception is in areas specifically designed for district heating, where access to the pipes was required. For example, large, older university campuses often have underground tunnels that follow the steam lines. These tunnels are great to explore, especially in cold climates when the days are short.

Ruins

Although ruins are not necessarily underground, exploring their dim or dark passages feels like a subterranean odyssey. Whether you are exploring the hidden catacombs of an abandoned factory, crawling inside the rusted belly of an old boiler of a shut-down power plant, descending a ladder deep into the darkness of a forgotten grain silo, crawling, along creaking catwalk (with a one-Mississippi, two-Mississippi, three-Mississippi, fou . . . , seconds drop to the faint splash below), or investigating the musty rooms of a haunted building, with every step you pass through fear to see what is revealed on the other side.

Outside Chico, California is an abandoned missile base from the 1960s where you can climb down a fifty-foot ladder inside a steel culvert to a whole world of intricate passageways. Some lead to the deep, echoing missile storage silos, while others lead to command rooms filled with archaic computer equipment and littered with technical documents.

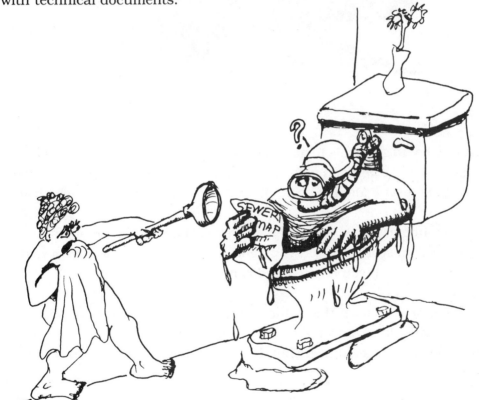

Ruins are the best places to find treasure. An excursion into dead and forbidden places turns us into Indiana Jones archaeologists. But remember, taking your chances and taking pictures are fine; taking anything else is theft.

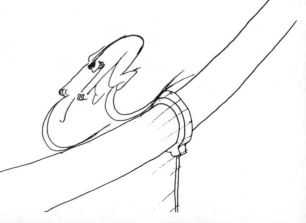

Technique

Not much specialized technique is required to explore subterranean urban environments.

Crawling

This is the self-evident technique of moving on hands and knees.

Mapping

The best way not to get lost is to do some mapping as you go. Mapping requires little more than making conscious note of the route that you are taking so that you can reverse it if necessary. Mapping can either be done on paper or in your head.

Intersections. Intersections are places where you make a choice about which direction to go. Keep track of which way you went through each intersection by noting the tunnels through which you entered and exited the intersection.

Curves. Make note of when the tunnel you are traveling curves and in which direction. You may not know how many degrees the tunnel is curving, especially if the turn occurs over a long distance. That doesn't matter, as long as you note that there is a curve.

Distance. You may want to note the distance between decision points or other points of reference. It is often difficult to tell distance underground and in the dark. Time is not a good measure unless you are moving at a consistent pace. Counting walking or crawling steps works well if you want a lot of detail and accuracy in your mapping effort.

Landmarks. Sometimes it is possible to see or hear something that will help you establish your location with respect to the world above. For example, you may be able to look up through a grating. Use this information to adjust your sense of orientation.

Lifting Manhole Covers

Professional subterranean workers lift manhole covers by placing a hooking device in the holes and lifting straight up. You may also be able to lift manhole covers by placing the end of an iron rod, like a crow bar, in one of the holes and pushing down on the other end off to the side. Longer bars make better levers. If you need to lift the manhole cover, be sure to keep your back straight to avoid injury.

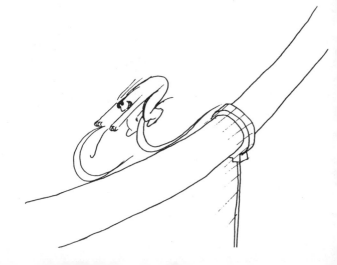

If you enter the underworld through a manhole, be sure to replace the cover over you both to avoid detection and to prevent someone else from accidentally coming through the same hole.

Safety and Special Risks

Of all the activities discussed in this book, subterranean exploration is one of the most dangerous. This is for several reasons:

A. Subterranean environments are themselves dangerous. They are not designed for human presence and often contain inherently harmful elements. For example, sewer systems contain deadly bacteria, lethal gasses, and areas without oxygen. Subways contain speeding trains and exposed high-voltage electric lines. General public utility vaults and tunnels may have natural gas leaks or exposed high-voltage electric wires.

B. It is easy to wander into a dangerous situation before you are prepared to handle it. No skills beyond walking and crawling are required for you to arrive at a situation that can kill you. It is unlike buildering, where, generally, the climber develops skills that lead him to precarious places and train him how to survive simultaneously.

C. There are no warnings. The dangers underground, like an absence of oxygen, are often undetectable through human sensory perception. Other dangers are detectable, but not within a time frame that will allow you to respond evasively. This is unlike the aboveground activities where you can clearly see when the risks start increasing.

Liquid Carrying Systems

Generally, the water found in drainage systems is polluted. It contains lead, oil, fecal matter, urine, and any garbage that happens to wash down the street. So don't drink it. Operating sewers, in particular, are deadly bacteria-infested environments.

Other dangers of liquid waste carrying systems include asphyxiation and drowning.

Transportation Tunnels

Transportation tunnels are filled with vehicles that are not expecting pedestrians, so stay out of their way or be run over. Many tunnels have built-in walkways, but in those that don't, ducking into an alcove or moving to another track can keep you out from under a train.

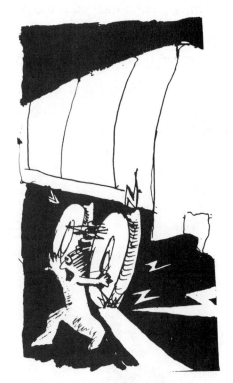

While you are in these tunnels, be careful not to touch the third rail or the wire that carries the power for the vehicle or you will fry immediately. People die that way every year.

When entering a transportation tunnel, watch to see if you are being watched. If you are in a public transportation tunnel, you are trespassing and subject to arrest.

Sometimes homeless people live in transit system stations and tunnels. If you are down there when the system is not operating, you may meet some. The people you meet may or may not be dangerous. Your best defense is to go about your adventure as though you belong there. Be polite, but do not get engaged in conversation unless you want to. Show no fear and display no signs of wealth.

Ruins

The major danger in a ruin is the decomposing structure itself. Watch for water damage and rust or the metal ladder you are climbing may disengage from the wall. Watch for sagging floors and ceilings as signs of an impending cave-in.

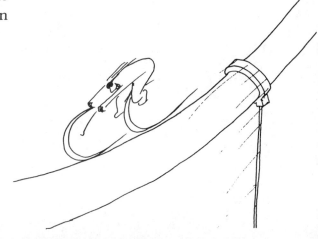

Etiquette

- If your underground adventure has been in any place unpleasant, have a good cleaning and change your clothing before proceeding to your next activity.

- If you meet homeless people living in the underworld, treat them courteously and with respect. You are passing through their house.

- Treasure found in ruins should be left for the next explorer to see. Many grave robbers collect more than they want by evoking the curses of the ancients whom they plunder.

Equipment

Light

Headlamps or flashlights are needed to explore dark places. Headlamps are preferable because they leave your hands free. Test your light before descending and consider carrying a backup.

Matches and candles are also useful if you are absolutely sure there is no combustible gas. Matches make a great emergency backup if your light fails. I make a habit of taking matches every time I leave a restaurant for the unexpected after-dinner adventure.

Protective Clothing

Rubber boots, gloves, and coveralls are recommended if you are going to explore places that may be wet or muddy.

Compass

A compass is useful for keeping track of your direction in a complex underground network.

Periscope

Periscopes are useful for looking out of drainage grates to get your bearings. A small dentist's mirror that can be poked through the holes in grates and manhole covers has been suggested as a good tool for orientation.

Special Safety Equipment

If you are going into an area where there is likely to be high concentrations of bacteria and little airflow, such as in sewers, it is best to carry working electronic gas sensing equipment and possibly oxygen. Contact your local department of public works, wastewater division, to find out where you can get these devices.

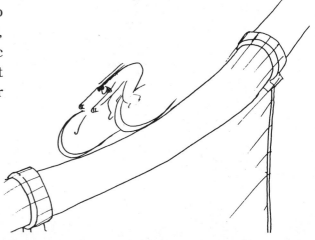

A Sub-Urban Float

"Sure," said Jim, "It was really wild. I'd be glad to tell you all about it. How about Wednesday, after work, over a couple of brews?"

We got off the phone. I could hardly wait. I was going to hear about one of the greatest **URBAN ADVENTURES** of all times, right from the source.

I already knew the story. Pablo had told me, at least all he could remember. But he wasn't there.

One year when there were really heavy rains, Jim and a couple of his rafting friends had floated down Strawberry Creek all the way to the Bay. Strawberry Creek starts in the Berkeley Hills and runs through the University of California campus. At the end of campus it gets channeled underground and runs for about five miles under the city of Berkeley.

They had dressed in wet suits and brought headlamps.

As they floated on the fast-moving current through the dark tunnel, storm drain tributaries added more water. There were small rapids. At one point they heard falling water. Before they knew it, they had dropped over a six-foot waterfall. The further they went, the less air space there was between the water and the pipe's ceiling. Soon the air space was just large enough for their heads.

"Did either of you guys check the outlet to see if there was a grate across it?" one of them asked.

No one had. Pablo told me that Jim had had visions of being forced through the grate like noodles from a pasta machine.

Nothing could be done. The current was too swift to swim against. They just kissed the ceiling of the pipe for their air and hoped for the best.

Wednesday after work Jim and I met at Houlihans.

"What kind of Irish bar is this with no Irish beer?" Jim asked.

"Good point," responded the waitress, "What do you want?"

"How about a Corona," said Jim.

Jim turned to me and said, "I did the run with this guy called 'Crazy Richard.' I can't remember his real name. We were both students at Cal. Crazy Richard was a math student and I was studying music at the time.

"It had been raining a lot that winter, and you know how it is with river types: as soon as water is flowing in the gutters, you start figuring out how you would run it.

"The rivers were high that year. Water was flowing over the top of Death Rock on the Stanislaus. We were river-crazy and ran everything we could. On weekends we would go to the Sierra or up to the Smith."

There was a twinkle in his eye and a touch of the self-assured madness of youth in his voice as he told how he ran every urban creek and flood control ditch he could find when he didn't have time to drive to rivers.

"Crazy Richard and I were on the Sproul Plaza bridge, looking at Strawberry Creek and watching it rain," he said.

"We figured we could run it if it just rained a little harder. It did. We decided to try it. Soon we were running with kayaks across campus for rain hats, looking for a place to put in.

"There was plenty of water, but the creek was so narrow that we couldn't turn around. We went over a few three- to four-foot man-made waterfalls. We had to back-paddle to play in the turbulence below them.

"Before long we were at the Sproul Plaza bridge. The creek mellowed and got wider. We played there for a long time and drew a crowd of spectators.

"The sun started poking through the clouds. The lure of the river drew us down stream.

"The creek narrowed again and I started wondering about what would happen when the creek went underground. I asked Crazy Richard. He didn't know. I imagined all kinds of horrible fates. I wondered how long I could back-paddle against the current and kept looking for places to take out.

"Then we heard that familiar sound of falling water. We back-paddled like crazy to slow our progress. In front of us the creek disappeared into a big hole. We back-paddled even harder, but the current pulled us further toward the hole. Soon we were on a grate, and the water plummeted below. We stood up and laughed at the anticlimactic finish."

"You mean that you never went underground?" I asked.

"No," he replied, "unless you want to count going under the Sproul Plaza bridge."

"That's amazing," I said. "Pablo told me a completely different story."

He laughed. "That's river lore for ya."

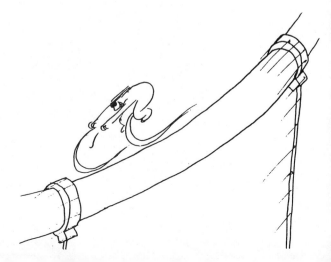

GOING HIGH

"Adventure starts anytime you move around a locked gate, climb over a fence, slide under barbed wire, or pass through barriers of restricted vision."
BODIVOODOO

A city is filled with towering edifices that define its looks, feel, and character much as a mountain range is defined by its precipices and jagged ridge lines. In both environments, some people are content to stand and stare in awe of the walls before them, while other people are driven to climb the most magnificent towers all the way to their tops.

Fear is cheap a few hundred feet off the ground. All you have to do is be there, exposed, with nothing but a lot of air below you, to feel your heart pounding in your ears, tongue dry and swollen inside your mouth, cold beads of sweat on your forehead, and fingers white and aching from gripping too hard at whatever is in your hand.

Going high may be easy or difficult. Sometimes it is as easy as climbing a ladder. Going high may have little risk; often it is unlikely that you will fall unless you let go. But the potential consequences of going high are always extreme: almost any fall will be fatal. Most **URBAN ADVENTURERS** back off the edge of high standard balletic buildering and occasionally use a mechanical backup to protect themselves in death-defying places.

Sometimes entire ascents are made with the use of mechanical wall-gripping devices. Climbs dependent on mechanical wall-scaling hardware are called aid climbs. Aid climbing is a technical solution to a climbing problem and is used when the objective is to get to the top any way you can. Aid climbing is particularly useful when a structure's surface lacks the features that would make buildering feasible, especially up high.

Going high is goal oriented. In your effort to get to the top and back down safely, there is no such thing as cheating.

The Medium

Towers

Towers are fun to climb because they are high, scary, and generally easy. Many towers come equipped with ladders, although access to these ladders may take some creative climbing because they are often locked and/or start high off the ground. Towers typically found in urban areas include water towers, communication towers, and smokestacks.

Bridges

Bridges are like trails through the air. Almost any bridge has some alternative way of crossing it that will make you dramatically aware of your position above the planet's surface. Sometimes the most exciting crossing is on the steel girders below the roadway. Sometimes the choice crossing is on the structural reinforcements above a roadway. The Golden Gate Bridge in San Francisco has suspension cables that can be climbed to supporting towers high above the roadway, which itself is high above the treacherous entrance to the San Francisco Bay.

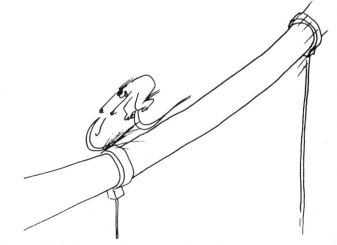

Monuments

Monuments are architectural testaments to our culture and its heros and therefore should definitely be climbed out of respect to the people and ideas they represent. Unfortunately, they usually are not climbed for two reasons: first, they are usually illegal to climb, which means that they would have to be climbed very fast; and second, they often have minimal surface features, which makes them very difficult to climb.

Two monuments that beg to be climbed, but, to my knowledge have not yet been ascended, are the Washington Monument in Washington, D.C. and the Gateway Arch in St. Louis, Missouri.

High-rise Buildings

Downtown high-rise buildings are the main arena for **URBAN ADVENTURERS** who like to scale human-made structures using aid. Most high-rise buildings cannot be climbed to the top using buildering techniques because they have no usable hand- or footholds. High-rise buildings tend to have extremely uniform exterior characteristics with features that may include small cracks between large surface plating segments like shallow, grooved, concrete expansion cracks, exterior window framing, and tracks used for window washing equipment. Exceptions to a building's uniform exterior often occur at the very bottom and the very top.

Technique

Overcoming a Debilitating Fear of Heights

Almost everyone has a fear of falling from high places. It is innate. It is the fear of heights that gives us that adrenalin rush whenever we are up high in an exposed or precarious position. The manifestation of that fear varies in individuals; some people have a healthy respect for the dangers associated with heights and take extra precaution, while others, who have a debilitating vertigo, feel like they will get sucked over the edge of any precipice and have been known to actually jump.

As a child adventurer I was terrified of heights, but the drive to climb trees was strong. I learned to never look down and to be very deliberate in all my actions. Paying attention to everything but the ground was the key.

If you are afraid of heights, don't think about the ground; rather, focus on your position and on your next move. If you want to look down to enjoy the view, look out rather than straight down. The best view is not directly below you anyway; it is on the horizon.

If you are downclimbing, it is fine to look down for your next hold, but don't focus on the ground. Remember, your eye cannot focus on something close, like the next foothold, and something far away, like the ground, at the same time. Take advantage of that limitation.

When you get really scared, like all climbers do, just take a moment to breathe deeply and relax. Shake out your hands and feet one at a time to get blood flowing through them. Don't rush; there is no time pressure. When you finish your cry, start to calm down, and are breathing deeply, think about your next move and make it. If you can't make the move, relax some more and then try again. All you have to do is one move at a time.

Some adventurers who are afraid of heights like to scare themselves on purpose. They climb to a high and exposed place. They secure themselves so that there is no way they can slip. Then they stare at the ground, letting the full impact of the exposure freak them out. This is a great way to get the adrenaline flowing and may help to desensitize you to heights.

A Running Self-Belay

There are times when you are going high that you may wish that you could be tied to something solid just in case you accidentally slip. Often this wish can be accomplished with a minimal amount of hardware by using a running self-belay. To belay means to hold or secure. In the climbing world, the term "on belay" usually means that someone is holding the rope you are attached to, so if you fall, the other person will catch you. To self-belay means to have rigged a device to catch yourself if you fall. A running self-belay is a mechanism that will move with you to protect you if you slip. A belay can be used to protect you during a single difficult move or an entire climb.

There are three types of running self-belays. (Roped belaying techniques are not discussed in this book because roped belaying is rarely done on building climbs or other **URBAN ADVENTURES.** For information about roped belaying, consult a textbook on rock climbing.)

The *sliding self-belay* is a short looped leash, attached to your harness, that goes around a long structural support running in the direction you are moving. Typically the support is a cable or a rail. The loop is designed to run freely along the support cable or rail. The leash loop is attached to itself, or back to your harness, using a carabiner so that the loop can quickly be detached and reattached at places where the supporting cable or rail is connected to the main structure. For added safety, two loop leashes can be used, so that one is always attached during loop readjustment at support connection points.

The sliding self-belay is often used by **URBAN ADVENTURERS** who are in slippery high places where the movement is more horizontal than vertical. It is a favored protection technique used by **URBAN ADVENTURERS** who scale the suspension cables on the Golden Gate Bridge.

Loose prusik knot

Tight prusik knot

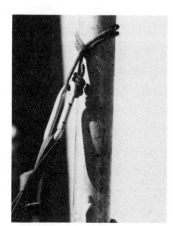

Prusik on a pole

The *prusik belay* is similar to the sliding self-belay except that the loop contains a prusik knot around the rail or cable, and the carabineer end of the leash is attached to the bottom of the prusik knot. A prusik knot will slide if it is loose but will not slide if it is tightened. The prusik belay is used when a sliding self-belay will not stop your fall. The more times the prusik is wrapped around the pole or cable the more it will want to grab and the less it will want to slide. It is most useful if you are climbing a long vertical cable or pole and often is attached only at times when you want to rest.

The *running anchor belay* uses a piece of climbing hardware attached to your harness to protect your moves on a vertical wall. After each climbing move you replace the piece of climbing hardware so that the next move will be protected. The running anchor belay is most effective in protecting your movement up continuous, uniform deep cracks on high-rise buildings. Sometimes more than one size of climbing hardware is necessary because even human-made cracks vary, especially over time. If you are going to rest by hanging from your running anchor belay, you should place more than one piece.

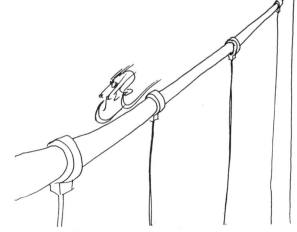

Aid Climbing

Just about any human-made or natural formation can be climbed using some type of aid technique. The only limiting factor is technical ingenuity.

Aid climbing technique is basically simple. Pieces of special climbing hardware are used to grip a wall. These can be hooks, camming devices, nuts, knots or any special devices designed to grip a particular wall. Small, light, flexible ladders called *étriers,* are attached to the wall-gripping hardware. The climber stands in the étriers. He moves up by placing progressively higher pieces of wall-gripping hardware, attaching another set of étriers, and moving onto the higher étrier. When his weight is on the higher piece of hardware, he can remove a lower one for use later. He proceeds by repeating the process.

Some aid techniques alter the surface being climbed. For example, riveting and placing expansion bolts require that holes be drilled into the wall being climbed. Placing pitons, bashies, and other hammer-driven implements chips the sides of cracks and holes. These destructive techniques permanently alter the surface of the structure being climbed and therefore will not be discussed in this chapter.

Aid placements on buildings are usually easy to make but not necessarily secure. I have had "friends" pop out of deep parallel concrete cracks unexpectedly.

Aid climbing in an urban environment is an engineering and endurance problem. Difficult aid climbing on rock requires a lot of creative ingenuity to make use of small and irregular features. The climber must make an engineering assessment for every move. Building features, on the other hand, are fairly consistent. Creativity is required to figure out how to move up the building in the first place, but once the problem is solved, the climber will likely make the same move, or the same series of moves, for the entire length of the climb. Typically, the surface feature being climbed is a crack. That crack will often run of the building's height, although it may vary in size. The streetlevel part of a building is the most likely section to be inconsistent. Overcoming the initial barriers is often the most difficult part of the climb. The very top of a building can also be a little tricky. Older buildings often have overhanging lips at the top. Most modern high-rise structures do not. Once the climber is at the base of the crack, he can make the same type of placement repeatedly until he is at the top. In essence, his creative challenge is to figure out how to make that one placement.

Aid climbing on high-rise buildings is the outsider's way to the top of corporate America.

Going Up Using Three Alternating Aid Placements

From a secure position:

1. Place a piece of climbing hardware with an attached étrier as high as you can. The ideal placement will be secure enough to jump up and down on without it moving or slipping. (When aid climbing on rock, the étrier is not usually attached to the climbing hardware before placement. The étrier may get in the way of the placement, or there may be some uncertainty about the actual piece of hardware to be used. This uncertainty should not occur on a building climb, because placements have little variance in their shape or size.)

2. Test the placement and step up. Pull down on the étrier and give it a little jerk. If the placement does not move, step into the étrier slowly and evenly until all of your weight is on the placement. Watch for shifting hardware. Do not lose your ability to return to the safe position while testing the placement, even if the new placement suddenly rips out. This can be done by keeping one foot and one hand on a previous placement, which you know is secure (i.e. the one you were standing on when you started). Try a little bounce. If the new placement still hasn't moved and appears secure, you are there. If it does move, find a secure placement.

Aid climbing. Note the three "friends" being used: two attached to étriers and one for backup tied into her harness.

3. Slide up your running anchor belay. Test it with a few downward yanks.

4. Reach down and remove the placement that you were standing on previously. Place it higher, test it, and stand on it. You are ready to repeat the whole process.

Following this procedure will mean that you always have at least two pieces of hardware connected to the building. This is a fast and safe way to proceed.

On noncontinuous aid climbs (for example if the holds are four feet apart), you can leapfrog using three étriers to maintain the same level of safety. When you are moving in the étriers, try to be smooth. Avoid any jerky movement that may dislodge the placement you are standing on.

When using either method, you should absolutely trust every placement. If you do not trust each placement implicitly you should either be using a rope technique or be climbing a different building.

Protection on an Aid Climb

Aid climbing is only safe when there is no way to fall. This means that you must choose a building that will not deteriorate, place aid climbing devices that provide a secure grip on the building, and make sure that you are securely connected to the hardware gripping the building.

Each piece of aid climbing hardware that is being used to grip the wall should be attached to your climbing harness with nylon webbing. If you happened to fall out of your étriers, you would then be caught by the wall-gripping hardware.

Aid climbing using a rope is not discussed in this book because it is rarely done on buildings. For information about roped aid climbing, consult a textbook on rock climbing.

Getting Down From an Aid Climb

Getting down from a building aid climb is not a major problem. If you climb a high-rise building, most likely you will be arrested, and get to ride down in the elevator with a police escort. If you do not get arrested you can try to get into the building through a roof door and ride the elevator without a police escort. You may also be able to get access to internal fire escape stairs. At the bottom when you exit, you will probably trip an alarm, so be prepared to run or get caught. (Repelling down is another option, though rarely used.)

Getting down from a monument may be difficult since there may not be access to the inside from the top. Work out your downclimbing technique before you go up. Getting rescued from the top of a monument may be both embarrassing and expensive.

Safety and Special Risks

1. Climbing communication towers may be a health risk when they are transmitting (which may be always). There are often high-voltage electric lines, and I personally would not like to climb near a microwave transmitter after hearing what the microwave oven did to the cat.

2. Beware of rusty ladders when climbing old towers. Rungs may break off in your hand.

3. Be careful when going over barbed-wire fences to get to towers. They are easy to climb with some practice. Watch for snagged clothing and be sure to have a recent tetanus shot.

4. On aid climbs, keep your climbing hardware system as simple as possible. Complexity only leads to mistakes. Eliminate unnecessary equipment beyond your basic safe system. Tie safety lines directly into your harness systems. Remember, every piece of equipment is just one more thing that can fail.

5. Keep every piece of equipment clipped to you at all times. First, if you drop something, it is gone and cannot be recovered. You lose access to it for the rest of the climb. Second, if you hit someone on the head with a piece of hardware dropped from high up, you will likely kill the person and be charged with manslaughter.

6. Beware of placing aids in bird drippings. The dry ones can crumble and the wet ones can be slippery.

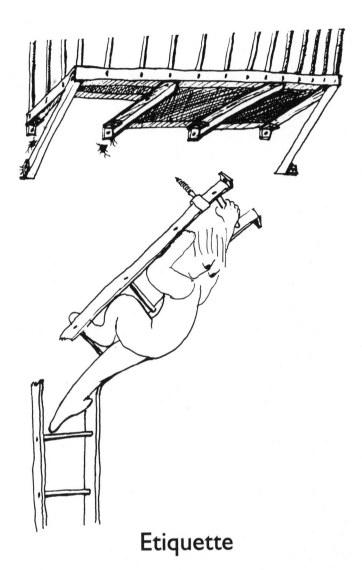

Etiquette

- Don't cut barbed-wire fences to get into towers. It is easy enough to climb over them or to look for places where other wild animals have tunneled under.

- If you are climbing a window-washing track, do not use one currently being used by window washers. You shouldn't get in their way. They are working and you are playing.

- If you drop something when climbing, yell to warn people down below.

- When you get hauled in for trespassing, etc., don't call your attorney, significant other, or mom at an unreasonable hour.

Equipment

Going high does not necessarily require special equipment. However, aid climbing may be a very equipment-intensive activity.

Harness

The primary purpose of a harness is to hold your body if you fall. Second, you may want a harness that is comfortable to sit in if you want to hang from aid placements. The simplest harness consists of one-inch tubular webbing wrapped around your waist three to five times and tied with a water knot. This is called a swami belt. Leg loops can be added to a swami belt to make it more comfortable. Most climbers prefer commercial harnesses. For building aid-climbs, a simple, easy-to-move-in harness is best.

Carabiner

A carabiner is a mechanical snapping link.

Looping Leash

A looping leash is a piece of rock-climbing–grade webbing or rope that is tied to your harness capable of holding at least one thousand pounds. The looping leash has to be long enough to loop around whatever you are using for your running belay and be secured to itself or back to your harness with a carabiner.

Wall-gripping Hardware

There are several types of wall-gripping hardware, including single and double camming devices, sliding wedges, and hooks that will not damage building exteriors. The best place to find this equipment is in a mountaineering store and other places that sell rock climbing hardware. You, as an **URBAN ADVENTURER,** may need to design special wall-gripping devices for special situations.

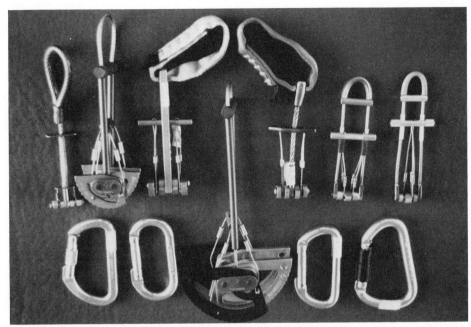

Assorted carabiners and camming wall-gripping hardware.

Étriers

Étriers are sling ladders. Commercial étriers are available, or you can easily make one. If you actually need the étrier to serve a ladder function, you may want to attach two étriers on each piece of hardware. If you are just standing in the same loops for the whole climb, you may want to build a special pair for the particular climb. If you make your own étriers, use one-inch–wide flat webbing. You can make the step by stitching the webbing or by tieing knots.

Clothing

Since most "going high" activities are illegal, I recommend stripes for day-time assents and informal dark evening wear for tower climbs at night. For monument and high-rise aid ascents, wear something you want to be photographed in since you will probably get arrested.

Shoes

Your same old sneakers are great for most "going high" adventures. For aid climbs, I recommend a firm sole for comfort and a rugged toe to resist abrasion. Standing in étriers can be painful in soft shoes or in bare feet.

An Upscale Adventure

The climber wasn't noticed until she passed the tenth floor. Then she was spotted by a wino in the park across the street who was howling at the sun.

First the SWAT team arrived. They wanted to shoot down the human fly. Then came the guy with a bullhorn. He was chosen because he had gotten his degree in psychology before joining the police force. He was always called in for suicide-prevention cases and cases in which junkies held people hostage. The fire department came next to set up a big catcher's mitt. The chief played coach and umpire, hoping to call strike.

A crowd started to form around the outside of the yellow barricade tape. Some kids ducked under to get a closer look and were chased off by a cop. Everyone was getting real excited.

"Crackle, skreetch, blather, blather skreetch," or something like that, said the guy on the bullhorn. It was impossible to make out the words. It was just a loud noise, like a garbage truck with blown bearings and a broken muffler farting down the street.

"Skreech. Come down, you are under arrest," said the bullhorn.

"Why?" I wondered from my grounded vantage point. She can't be breaking in. None of the windows will open. What's the damage? Where is the crime?

People started to appear in the windows, straining to get a view of the climber. Anything beat sitting in front of a computer screen.

"This is your last chance, or you will be resisting arrest," said the bullhorn.

The climber moved up the vertical crack, not fast, but steadily. She made the same move over and over again in her colored sling ladders.

The crowd poured into the street, blocking traffic. More police arrived to control the crowd.

She had a few more stories to go.

The guy with the bullhorn and half a dozen SWAT team members headed for the front door. They were prepared. She was going to be arrested. They would not let the climber jump to her death. They would not let her shoot her way out.

She neared the top.

ENDING 1

The heads of an un-welcoming committee appeared over the edge.

The heads moved back as she approached the top. People cheered. The climber reached for the summit. The SWAT team lunged for her. She jumped backward and flew off the wall.

People screamed at the plummeting body. The heads reappeared at the top. Every uniform reached for a radio and stared as the stone kite with the long tail dropped toward the ground.

A parachute opened. The climber aimed for the center of the park. The people below roared and raised their hands like kids trying to catch a fly ball over the left field fence.

The police tried to move to the center of the hero's welcome but were stopped by a swarm of other people who had the same idea. The climber landed. The canopy floated down. Chaos and euphoria ruled. No one was arrested for the evening news.

ENDING 2

The heads of an un-welcoming committee appeared over the edge. The climber reached for the summit. One member of the SWAT team reached to help her with a bruisingly firm grip.

She was booked for trespassing, fined five hundred dollars, and put on six months probation. Her ascent was a forty-five-second feature on the local evening news.

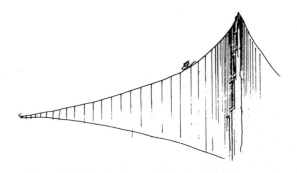

MISCELLANEOUS

"Creativity is the only limit to possibility."
BODIVOODOO

Adventures are as numerous and varied as the crystal patterns for snowflakes. Unconceived **URBAN ADVENTURES** are waiting to be born. That spark of madness that lucidly reveals our essential human nature seeks expression. It is not enough to hunt the wooly mammoth once you dream that you can ride it.

This chapter contains three **URBAN ADVENTURE** activities that do not require extensive explanation.

Rappelling

Rappelling is a technique used to descend steep rock or ice faces by sliding down a rope. Most rappellers use a mechanical braking device attached to the harness to control the speed of their descent. In urban environments, it is possible to rappel off buildings, bridges, towers, and so on.

Rappels can be done off either a single or double rope. Single-rope rappels are sometimes used when it is easy to return to the top of the building and recover the rope. Double-rope rappels are used when you need to pull the rope down after you have completed the rappel.

Technique

1. Set up an anchor. The rope should be attached to an object that will not break or move when force is exerted on it. Usually a nylon sling rope (one-inch

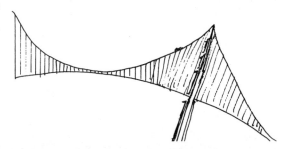

tubular webbing) is attached to the actual anchor. I try to have a least three completely independent anchor points. I use double slings and double carabiners. For a single-rope rappel, the rope can be attached to the sling with carabiners. For a double-rope rappel, the ropes can be run through the slings or carabiners so that they can be pulled through after the rappel is completed. The sling should be positioned so that the rope does not go over any sharp or abrasive surfaces. Carabiners should be positioned so that their gates open on opposite sides.

2. Set up the rope. Uncoil the rope into a loose pile. Make sure the rope is attached to the anchor. Then throw the free end(s) off the side of the structure. Sometimes it is better to feed the free end(s) down the wall. If there are two ends, make sure they both reach the bottom.

3. Put on the harness and attach the brake system to the rope. The harness should have leg loops.

Carabiner brake system and figure-8 brake system.

4. Put on the brake and lean back over the edge of the building. You will find that if you do not have some slack in the rope, you will have to feed the rope through the brake in order to move over the edge. To apply the brake, hold the rope tightly below the brake. For additional friction, run the free (or bottom) end of the rope behind your back. It is common for beginning rappellers to want to grab the rope above the brake. This may seem intuitively correct, but it is very dangerous. If you start to slip, you can only stop yourself by applying the rope brake. *Never let go with the brake hand.*

5. Lean back until you are perpendicular to the wall, then start walking down the wall backward. It is not difficult to rappel. You can be an expert the first time you try it. As you get more confident, you can start walking back and forth sideways on the wall and pushing yourself away from the wall with your feet.

Equipment

Rope

Some type of climbing rope is usually used. Make sure that your rope is long enough for the rappel. Also make sure that your rope is in good condition, without excessive abrasion, worn places, or cuts. Keep it that way by not running it over sharp edges. Check the rope after each rappel for signs of damage. Rappelling too fast can burn your rope.

Brake

This can be a figure-8 descender, a carabiner system, or another device.

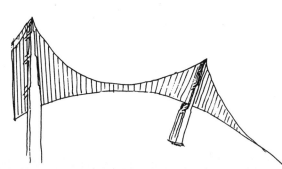

Harness

This can be a commercial climbing harness or one made from nylon webbing.

Slings to Attach the Rope to the Anchor

Riding on the Tops of Elevators

Many elevators have trap doors in their ceilings for emergency exits. These doors can generally be removed by unscrewing four bolts. Once on top of the elevator car, you can replace the trap door and spend hours riding up and down in the exposed shaft.

An alternative way of entering the ride is to stop between floors, force the upper elevator doors open, and climb directly onto the top of the elevator. Expect the alarm to ring when you stop the elevator.

If you decide to go for a top-of-the-elevator ride, do not stick your head or hands over the edge of the car. As the elevator goes up and down, so do counterweights. A counterweight coming down on your head while you are going up can be very painful or deadly.

Parachuting in an Urban Environment

Rumor has it that parachuting off of major urban features may be the next craze. It is an adventure waiting to happen. If you are inclined to try it, be fully experienced in fixed platform parachute jumping. Expect devious wind currents in the urban canyons.

Happy Adventuring!

GLOSSARY

Aid climbing: Means of ascending a building (or rock wall) by climbing on artificial holds, made of climbing hardware, placed by a climber.

Anchor: A wall or pole that a chain or cable is attached to.

Belay: To secure oneself to an anchor point with a rope, carabiners, and slings as a means of protection in case of a fall.

Bouldering: The act of climbing on boulders.

Buildering: The act of climbing on buildings.

Carabiner: Snap link used for climbing.

Center dynamics: The long, even swing motion found when walking on the center of a slack chain or cable.

Chimneying: Climbing sandwiched between two walls by applying outward pressure against both walls.

Counterbalancing: Moving one thing to balance another. Often refers to staying in balance by moving body appendages to counter the effects of leaning in an opposite direction.

Crag: Rock outcropping used as a climbing area.

Drafting: Riding a bicycle in the air pocket created by a moving vehicle.

Edging: Using the edge of your foot to stand on a small foothold.

End dynamics: The short, choppy movements experienced while walking on a chain or a cable near its anchor points.

Étriers: Ladders for aid climbing, usually made out of nylon webbing.

Harness: A strong nylon cage around your body—to which a rope and other safety hardware can be attached—designed to hold you safely if you fall.

Holds: The points where you hold onto a climbing wall. Holds can be either footholds or handholds, depending on how they are used.

Jamming: Wedging a hand or foot into a crack or hole.

Layback: A climbing technique that relies on opposing pressure between the hands and feet. The feet push outward and the hands pull inward.

Manteling: A climbing technique that is used to get on top of a relatively horizontal surface.

Popping a wheely: Lifting the front tire of a bicycle off the ground. Ask any ten-year-old for a demonstration.

Problem or Climbing Problem: A section of a climb that may be particularly interesting or difficult.

Prusik knot: A way of wrapping a thin piece of rope or nylon webbing around a thicker rope, cable, or pole so that the thin piece of rope will not slip when weight is applied to it.

Put-in: Where you put the boat in the water at the start of a river trip.

Running self-belay: A self-belay that moves up a climb with the climber.

Self-belay: A method of protecting oneself using climbing hardware in the event of a fall.

Shielding: When a bicyclist uses vehicles to protect him/herself from other potentially menacing vehicles, especially at intersections.

Stemming: The climbing technique of stretching a leg out to use a foothold to the side.

Take-out: Where you take the boat out of the water at the end of a river trip.

Traversing: Moving across a climbing wall.

T-SHIRT BACK TEXT: "Adventure starts anytime you pass through barriers of restricted vision."
THE BODIVOODOO *The Urban Adventure Handbook*

The Urban Adventure T-shirt is printed black on high quality white 100% cotton T-shirts, in sizes Large and Extra-Large.

To order Urban Adventure T-shirts send a check or money order payable to Urban Adventure and mail to:

Urban Adventure
P.O. Box 9221
Berkeley, CA 94709

PLEASE SEND ME:

Numbers(s): _____ Large _____ Extra-Large

$ _____ Total for T-shirts (cost: $12.00 per T-shirt)

$ _____ Shipping Charges (@ $2.00 for first T-shirt; $0.50 for each additional T-shirt)

$ _____ California residents please include appropriate sales tax (6% - 7.5%)

$ _____ Total Amount Enclosed

Please remember to include your name and address.